STUDIES IN THE UK ECONOMY

The UK labour market

The UK labour market

Leslie Simpson
and
Ian Paterson
Heriot-Watt University
Edinburgh

Series Editor
Bryan Hurl
Head of Economics, Harrow School

Heinemann Educational Publishers
Halley Court, Jordan Hill, Oxford OX2 8EJ

MADRID   ATHENS   PARIS
FLORENCE   PRAGUE   WARSAW
PORTSMOUTH NH   CHICAGO   SAO PAULO
SINGAPORE   TOKYO   MELBOURNE   AUCKLAND
IBADAN   GABORONE   JOHANNESBURG

First published in 1995

99 98 97 96 95
10 9 8 7 6 5 4 3 2 1

British Library Cataloguing in Publication Data
A catalogue record for this book is available from the British Library

ISBN 0 435 33030 6

Typeset and illustrated by TechType, Abingdon, Oxon.
Printed and bound in Great Britain by Clays Ltd, St Ives plc

Acknowledgements

We would like to record our thanks to Pat Chrystal and Graeme Lewis from Heriot-Watt University for word-processing and the production of diagrams repectively. We are also indebted to Bryan Hurl for his support, guidance and editorial skills.

The publishers would like to thank the following for permission to reproduce copyright material: Associated Examining Board for the questions on pp. 26, 36, 45–7, 63, 84–7; CSO for the extract from *Social Trends*, 1991, on p. 13, Crown copyright, reproduced by the permission of the Controller of HMSO and the Central Statistical Office; the Department of Employment for the statistics from *New Earnings Survey* used in Figures 10 and 11 on pp. 24, 25 and Table A on p. 28; © *The Economist*, London, for the extracts on pp. 22, 56–7, 64; *Financial Times* for the statistics used in Figures A, B and D on pp. 84, 85; © *The Guardian* for the extracts on pp. 43 and 70 and the statistics used in Figure E on p. 86; Her Majesty's Stationery Office for the statistics from *Employment Gazette* used in Table 1 on p. 3, Figures A and B on p. 27, Table 2 on p. 35, Table A on p. 37 and Figure 18 on p. 81, Crown copyright is reproduced with the permission of the Controller of HMSO; IPPR/Rivers Oram Press for statistics taken from *Paying for Inequality* by Andrew Glyn and David Miliband, used in Figure 8 on p. 20; Douglas McWilliams and Mark Pragnell for the article on p. 54; Northern Examinations and Assessment Board for the questions on pp. 45, 71, 76, 84; Oxford and Cambridge Schools Examination Board for the questions on pp. 12, 37–8, 63, 76; Oxford University Press for the statistics from *Unemployment: Macroeconomic Performance and the Labour Market* by Layard, Nickell and Jackman, used in Figure 17 on p. 61; *Private Eye* for the cartoons by Les Barton, p. 58, and McLachlan, p. 69; © Times Newspapers Ltd, 1993/1994/1995, for the extracts from *The Times* on pp. 23, 72 and the statistics used in Figure C on p. 85 and Table A on p. 87; University of Cambridge Local Examinations Syndicate for the questions on pp. 26, 27–8, 37, 45, 76–7; University of London Examinations and Assessment Council for the questions on pp. 12–13, 26, 45, 63–5, 84; University of Oxford Delegacy of Local Examinations for the question on p. 12, 72; Welsh Joint Education Committee for the question on pp. 37, 63; The Wiltshire Times Series for the extracts from *The Wiltshire Times* on pp. 45–6; The World Bank for the extract from the *World Development Report*, 1991, on p. 77.

The publishers have made every effort to contact the correct copyright holders. However, if any material has been incorrectly acknowledged, the publishers would be happy to make the necessary arrangements at the earliest opportunity.

Contents

Preface

Studies in the UK labour market are the core of modern economics. The new syllabuses ratified by the SCAA reflect this fact. Indeed, some examination boards feature the labour market as an optional special choice subject.

This addition to the series covers all the expressed components outlined by the boards. The text is not jargonized: look not for '*hysteresis*' ...

Bryan Hurl
Series Editor

Introduction

A number of topics in the area of labour economics have been explored by other books in this series. However, this is the first time that one volume has been devoted to a wide range of micro- and macroeconomic labour market issues. In writing this book we have been conscious of the increased importance of the labour market in revised examination syllabuses. Consequently, we trust this will prove a useful addition to *Studies in the UK Economy*.

Chapter 1 outlines the different types of labour market that exist and discusses the supply and demand for labour. On the supply side, the distinction between the number of people supplying labour services and the number of hours of labour supplied is developed. On the demand side, the importance of the firm as the main employment unit is stressed.

Chapter 2 examines the economic theory of wage determination in competitive and non-competitive labour markets and discusses the reasons why wages differ between individuals, firms, industries and occupations.

Chapter 3 considers the role of trade unions and their effects on wages, employment and productivity. It also examines their growing powers during the 1970s and the controls imposed on them since 1979.

Chapter 4 tackles the controversial issue of minimum wage legislation. The effect of minimum wages on employment is analysed and the abolition of wages councils discussed.

Chapter 5 is mainly concerned with unemployment. It explains the alternative approaches to labour market equilibrium in the economy as a whole adopted by different schools of economic thought and the policy implications that result from them. Particular attention is paid to the concept of the natural rate of unemployment.

Chapter 6 highlights the problems of mismatch between the supply and demand for labour when industrial restructuring occurs. The importance of vocational education and training provision is emphasized.

Chapter 7 discusses the UK government's decision to opt out of the social chapter of the Maastricht treaty on European union.

Chapter 8 considers some recent developments in the UK labour market. It examines trends in pay determination, the use and deployment of labour, employment in manufacturing and services, female employment and trade union organization and argues that there is much greater diversity in the labour market today than there was in the past.

Chapter One
Labour markets

'The labour market is a very special kind of market.' Sir John Hicks

Economics textbooks often refer, as the title of this one does, to a nation's labour market. It is normally acknowledged, however, that within a country there are a whole host of labour markets which overlap and interconnect.

- **Local labour markets:** In practice employers recruit much of their labour from the localities close to their workplaces and normally within daily travelling distance. In order to recruit local labour, employers advertise in local newspapers and at the local job centre, and may make use of the services of an employment agency. Similarly, job seekers interested in locally available employment will use the same channels of information. There may be several overlapping local labour market areas in a big city. In a rural area small communities may depend upon a concentration of employment opportunities in a larger town.
- **Occupational labour markets:** The more skilled an individual is the more concerned he or she will be to find a job which makes use of those skills. Such an individual will be interested in the employment opportunities within his or her occupation. The information channels operating in an occupational labour market include national newspapers, technical and professional journals and, at a more informal level, personal contacts within the occupation. In geographical terms an occupational labour market may be national or even international.
- **Industrial labour markets:** Some industries, such as coal mining, employ workers who are highly specific to the industry in question and therefore it is possible to identify a third type of labour market, namely an industrial labour market. However, it is more common for an industry to use various types of labour which are also employed in a wide range of other industries. Electricians, for example, are employed in several different industries including engineering, shipbuilding, electrical contracting and electricity supply. It is, therefore, the occupational rather than the industrial link which is of greater importance to most specialized and skilled workers.

In examining a labour market, both the supply and demand sides of it must be considered. We begin by discussing labour market supply. *This is the quantity of labour, measured in labour hours, that people are willing to supply in a certain period of time.* Taking the size of the population as given, the amount of labour supplied in a particular period is a function of two variables:

- the number of persons engaged in or seeking employment (the supply of workers)
- the number of hours of work that each individual is willing to supply (the supply of labour hours).

The supply of workers

The number of persons willing to work as a proportion of the total population is known as the **labour force participation rate**. Such people are referred to as the *economically active* component of the population, or the *workforce*, and consist of two groups:

- those in employment (either employees or self-employed persons)
- those who are not in employment but who are actively seeking work (that is, those who are registered as unemployed).

In the UK, the estimated population in 1993 was 58 million, giving an estimated labour force participation rate of 49 per cent. Table 1 shows the employment statistics on which this latter estimate is based.

Table 1 The UK workforce, 1993 (millions)

Workforce in employment	25.3
Workforce unemployed	2.9
Total workforce	28.2

Source: *Employment Gazette*, December 1994

Perhaps the most important determinant of the labour force participation rate is the **age structure** of the population. In order to allow for the influence of this, we can calculate the labour force participation rate *for those of working age*, i.e. those over the statutory minimum school-leaving age, but below the normal retirement age. Over the period 1975–92, the participation rate of men of working age fell from 93 per cent to 87 per cent. However, the most significant change that took place over this period was the rise in the participation rate of married women from 59 per cent to 73 per cent. The rate for unmarried women remained the same at 73 per cent.

It is possible to distinguish between regular and occasional labour force participants. This distinction, based essentially on the degree of attachment of people to the labour force, has been formalized by dividing those who supply labour into two groups – **primary and secondary workers.** *Primary workers are those with a high degree of attachment to the labour force*, principally the main breadwinners of families whose labour-force attachment is unlikely to change either because of changes in family circumstances or in the general economic situation. *Secondary workers have a lower degree of labour-force attachment* and include:

- women who move into and out of the labour force in response to changes in marital status, domestic responsibilities, family income and job opportunities
- men who do not want to work continuously and who can afford not to
- young people who move into and out of the labour force whilst completing their education
- handicapped people and senior citizens who seek or hold temporary employment.

The distinction between primary and secondary workers not only enables us to distinguish between a permanent and a transitory element in the labour force, but it also suggests that *we should consider the family or the household, rather than the individual, as the main decision-making unit with respect to labour force participation decisions.*

Moreover, *decisions to participate in labour-market activity cannot be taken independently of competing demands on people's time.* Time has an opportunity cost, since time spent in one activity might have been spent doing something else. The opportunity cost of spending time on activities such as leisure and housework, for which there is no monetary return, is the wages payable had the time been used for labour-market activity. If there is no demand for the labour services that could have been provided, the opportunity cost will be zero. However, for a full-time housewife who could obtain paid employment, the opportunity cost of remaining a housewife could be substantial.

Decisions about who enters the labour force, and the associated question of how many hours to work, are typically made in the context of the household and as part of a wider decision about the optimal allocation of its members' time between alternative uses such as leisure, education and household work (including cooking, cleaning and childcare).

The supply of labour hours

The question of the supply of labour hours is related to the allocation of an individual's time between different activities. It may be argued that as hourly wage rates rise it becomes increasingly expensive for individuals to take time off work. The cost, in terms of wages forgone, of leisure and other unpaid activities increases. We might then expect a worker to be willing to supply more hours of work as rates of pay rise and substitute work for leisure. The supply curve of labour hours of such an individual would be positively sloped (rising from left to right), there being a substitution of work for leisure as wage rates increase. Economists call this a **substitution effect**.

On the other hand, one could argue that the higher the hourly rate of pay, the greater would be total earnings from a given number of hours of work. Since a person with a higher income is likely to spend more on consumption activities, many of which are time-consuming, he or she may be tempted to forgo some potential additional income by working fewer hours and allocating more time to leisure and other unpaid activities. So a rise in wage rates might cause some people to trade off additional income, in the form of hours of work, against leisure and other non-paid activities. The supply curve of labour hours of this type of individual would be negatively inclined (rising from right to left), with a reduction in hours supplied as wage rates increase. Economists call this an **income effect**.

These two arguments suggest completely different supply curves of labour hours. *As wage rates rise the substitution effect makes people want to work more and the income effect makes them want to work less.* Economic theory does not enable us to predict what will happen in practice since either effect could dominate. It is, nevertheless, reasonable to assume that the substitution effect will be of relatively greater importance at low levels of income than at high ones. At low income levels any rise in wage rates is likely to act as an incentive for a worker to work longer hours to increase his or her present earnings. However, at comparatively high wage rates the income effect may become dominant, making the individual's supply of labour hours (SLH) curve bend over and slope backwards.

This is illustrated in Figure 1, in which the effects of a rising income and an increasing opportunity to devote more time to leisure pursuits result in the income and substitution effects eventually cancelling each other out at a wage rate of W_1. At wage rates below W_1 the substitution effect is greater than the income effect, resulting in an increase in the supply of labour hours when wages rise. At wage rates above W_1 the income effect predominates and the supply of labour hours falls as wages rise, although

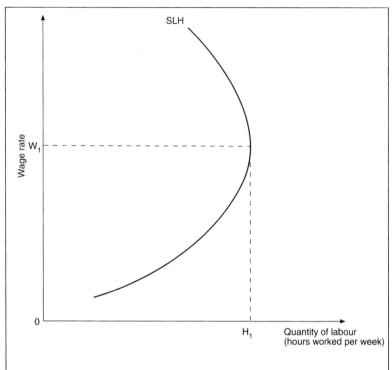

Figure 1 A backward-bending supply curve of labour hours

total income may still be increasing. The inverse relation between wage rates and hours worked that is commonly observed in cross-section empirical studies appears to support this hypothesis, but hours worked are determined by demand-side as well as supply-side forces.

Few people, other than the self-employed, can vary their supply of labour hours at will. Most have fixed hours of work to allow efficient work methods to be organized. Workers who are constrained by a standard working week – or any other arrangement which restricts their freedom to work the number of hours they would otherwise choose – may, however, overcome the constraint to some extent at least. For example, those who want to work more hours than they are offered by one employer may take a second job in the evenings or at weekends and eventually get a job in a company which offers plenty of overtime. On the other hand, those workers who want to work less hours than are required by their employers may resort to occasional or even regular **absenteeism** and eventually obtain a part-time job.

UK WORKERS' HOURS

Recently published European Union (EU) data indicates that whilst the trend in other EU countries is towards a shorter working week, in the UK the average number of hours worked per week, including overtime, rose from 42.3 in 1983 to 43.4 in 1992. The increase is the result of:

- high levels of overtime worked

- increased work loads of managerial and professional employees.

UK workers put in more hours per week, on average, than workers in any other EU country. Portugal is next highest with 41.3 hours whilst Belgium is the lowest with 38.2.

The market supply of labour

A labour market supply curve is obtained by adding together, horizontally, the labour supply curves of all those individuals participating in the market. Even though some individuals may have backward-bending labour supply curves, the labour market supply curve (SL) will be positively sloped. Such a curve is illustrated in Figure 2. As wage rates rise the quantity of labour supplied will increase. There are two reasons for this:

- some workers will wish to work more hours, substituting work for leisure
- more people will enter the labour force or switch from another labour market.

The firm's demand for labour

Economists regard the firm as the main decision-making unit when considering the demand for labour. Firms do not hire labour for the satisfaction of having employees, the way consumers purchase goods and services. *Workers are hired because they help to produce goods for consumers or other firms.* The firm's demand for labour is therefore said to be a **derived demand** because it is derived from the demand for the product or service that labour helps to produce.

A firm wishing to maximize its profits will produce additional output as long as the marginal cost of so doing is not greater than the marginal revenue obtained from selling the extra output. In the same way, a firm aiming at maximizing its profits will hire additional units of labour provided that the addition to total cost thereby incurred is not greater than the addition to total revenue obtained from the sale of the output produced by the extra labour.

7

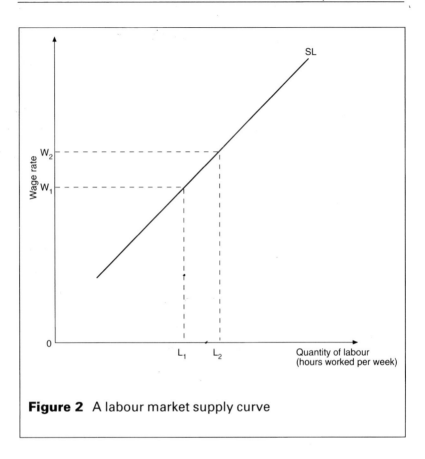

Figure 2 A labour market supply curve

In the short run the firm's stock of capital equipment will be fixed. As additional units of labour are employed output will rise. The increase in output produced by the employment of one extra unit of labour is called the **marginal physical product of labour**. Initially the marginal physical product of labour will rise as more workers are employed because of the advantages of the division of labour. However, as more and more labour is employed with the stock of capital equipment fixed, the marginal physical product of labour will start to fall because of the **law of diminishing marginal returns**.

A marginal physical product curve (MPPL) is shown in Figure 3. *The precise shape of this curve depends on the technical conditions of production.* The more advanced the technology being used the sharper the reduction in labour's marginal productivity tends to be because after a certain amount of labour is hired there is little that additional employees can do to increase output.

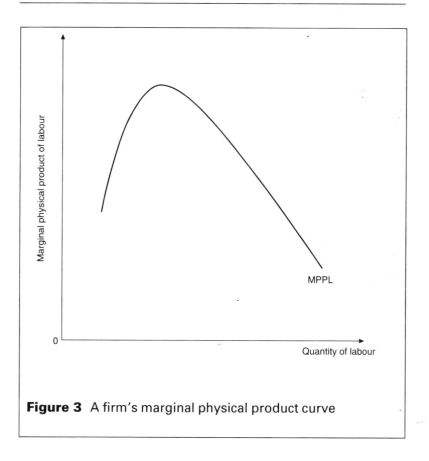

Figure 3 A firm's marginal physical product curve

In the same way that we can measure the marginal physical product of labour as the addition to total output that results from hiring an additional unit of labour, we can measure the addition to total revenue obtained from the sale of that extra output. This is called the **marginal revenue product of labour**. If the firm sells its product in a perfect market, all units of output can be sold at the same price – the firm does not have to drop the price in order to sell a greater output – and the marginal revenue product is equal to the marginal physical product multiplied by the price of the product. As the quantity of labour employed increases, the marginal physical product of labour will eventually fall, causing the marginal revenue product of labour to fall.

Suppose that employing an extra unit of labour enables a firm to increase output by ten units a day, each of which can be sold for £5. The marginal revenue product of labour is, therefore, £50 per day. Whether or not the firm hires the extra unit of labour depends on the wage rate. If the wage rate is less than £50 a day the firm would be able to add more to total revenue than the additional unit of labour adds to total costs and profits would rise. If it costs more than £50 a day to hire the extra unit of labour, the addition to total costs would be greater than the addition to total revenue and profits would fall. If it costs exactly £50 a day to hire the extra unit of labour, the addition to total costs and total revenue would be the same and profits would be unchanged. *So it is advantageous for a firm to hire labour up to and including that unit which adds the same amount to total revenue and total costs, that is where the marginal revenue product of labour is equal to the wage rate.*

Figure 4 illustrates a firm's marginal revenue product of labour curve (MRPL), *the downward sloping part of which is its demand curve for labour because it shows the amount of labour the firm will seek to employ at different wage rates.* If the wage rate is W_1, the profit-maximizing firm would hire E_1 units of labour – the level at which the wage (the cost of hiring an extra unit of labour) is equal to the marginal revenue product of

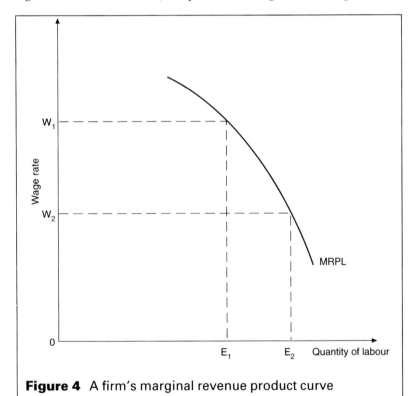

Figure 4 A firm's marginal revenue product curve

labour. However, if the wage rate is reduced to W_2, the firm would hire E_2 units of labour, since at that level of employment the marginal revenue product of labour would be equal to the new wage rate.

In the long run a firm can alter its inputs of capital as well as labour and the demand for labour depends on the price of labour relative to the price of capital. *When more than one factor of production is variable the marginal revenue product curve is no longer the firm's labour demand curve.* The marginal revenue product of labour shows what happens to revenue as labour inputs vary while capital inputs are fixed. Once it is possible to vary both labour and capital, a change in the price of either will result in a substitution between the two factors with more of the now relatively cheaper factor being purchased even if the firm's total output remains the same.

- If the wage rate increased while the cost of capital remained unchanged, the firm would eventually switch to a more capital-intensive method of production.
- If labour became relatively cheaper because of a substantial increase in the cost of capital equipment, the firm would in time switch to a more labour-intensive technique.

The firm's demand curve for labour will, therefore, be more elastic in the long run than in the short – how much more elastic depends on the ease with which capital can be substituted for labour. The easier such substitution is the greater the elasticity of demand for labour will tend to be.

The market demand for labour

A labour market demand curve can be constructed by adding together, horizontally, the demand for labour curves of each of the firms operating in the market. However, an allowance has to be made for any change in the price of the product and, consequently, the marginal revenue product of labour as the wage rate changes for the market as a whole. The market demand curve for labour will show that the market demand for labour increases as the wage rate falls.

Conclusion

The labour market is a very special kind of market. In a labour market the goods being traded are the services of men and women, who are active and not passive agents, with their own views on the buying and utilising of their services. In addition, the part played in labour markets by trade unions, employers' organizations and the government is extremely important as we shall see in subsequent chapters.

```
┌─────────────────────────────────────────────────────────────┐
│                        KEY WORDS                              │
│                                                               │
│  Local labour markets          Income effect                 │
│  Occupational labour markets    Absenteeism                   │
│  Industrial labour markets      Derived demand                │
│  Labour force participation     Marginal physical product     │
│    rate                           of labour                   │
│  Age structure                  Law of diminishing marginal   │
│  Primary and secondary            returns                     │
│    workers                      Marginal revenue product      │
│  Substitution effect              of labour                   │
│                                                               │
└─────────────────────────────────────────────────────────────┘
```

Reading list

Anderton, A., Unit 7 in *The Student's Economy in Focus*, Causeway Press, annual.

Beardshaw, J., Chapter 20 in *Economics – A Student's Guide*, 3rd edn, Pitman, 1992.

Economics and Business Education Association, Unit 15 in *Core Economics*, Heinemann Educational, 1995.

Stanlake, G.F., and Grant, S., *Introductory Economics*, 6th edn, Longman, 1995.

Essay topics

1. Explain the role of marginal revenue product in the theory of wage determination. To what extent does this account for wage levels in (a) the private sector, (b) the public sector? [8, 12 marks]
   [University of Oxford Delegacy of Local Examinations 1994]

2. (i) What are income and substitution effects? [10 marks]
   (ii) Show how these may be used to explain how a change in wage rates affects an individual's choice between work and leisure. [15 marks]
   [Oxford & Cambridge Schools Examination Board 1994]

Data Response Question 1

Aspects of the labour force

This task is based on a question set by the University of London Examinations and Assessment Council in 1995. Study the charts in Figures A and B and answer the questions.

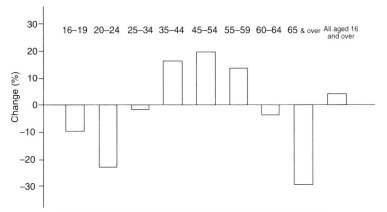

Figure A Changes in the British labour force, by age, 1989–2001

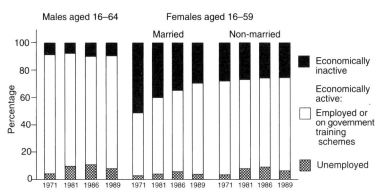

Figure B British population of working age, by sex and economic status, 1971–89 (adapted from *Social Trends*, 1991)

1. What is meant by 'the population of working age'? [2 marks]
2. (a) With reference to Figure A, identify the projected change in the age structure of the labour force between 1989 and 2001. [2 marks]
   (b) How are such projections arrived at? [2 marks]
   (c) Identify one problem in making such projections. [2 marks]
3. Analyse the likely economic effects of the changes shown in Figure A. [6 marks]
4. Using Figure B, explain the likely reasons for the changes in the proportion of the population which was economically *inactive* between 1971 and 1981. [3 marks]
5. What does this type of data contribute to an understanding of trends in unemployment? [3 marks]

Chapter Two

Wage determination

'Wage rates differ enormously.' Paul Samuelson

In an economist's model, wages are determined by the interaction of the labour market supply and demand curves. However, the theory of wage determination differs for different types of labour market. We will examine two cases:

- the first is a perfectly competitive labour market
- the second is a monopsony.

In both cases the assumption is made that employers are profit maximizers and employees are homogeneous. In reality, the employees in a particular labour market are not homogeneous, not least because of differences in education and training which will directly affect skill levels and productivity. This and other reasons for wage differentials will be investigated later in the chapter.

Perfectly competitive labour markets

The model of the perfectly competitive labour market assumes that there are a large number of employers and employees. Figure 5(a) illustrates the interaction of the labour market supply curve (SL) and demand curve (DL), giving a market equilibrium wage rate at W_1 and quantity of labour at L_1. As the firms in this labour market are perfectly competitive employers of labour, the labour supply curve for each firm (FSL) will be perfectly wage elastic. Thus all the firms can employ as much labour as they wish at the market wage rate W_1, which is the marginal cost of labour. As Figure 5(b) demonstrates, for each firm the profit maximizing level of employment will be achieved when the firm's demand for labour – the marginal revenue product of labour schedule (MRPL) – is equal to the firm's supply of labour. The quantity of labour employed by the firm is E_1.

The same analysis applies regardless of the structure of the product market in which the firm is operating. *It makes no difference whether the firm is a monopoly, perfectly competitive, or operating under conditions of imperfect competition.* As long as the labour market is itself

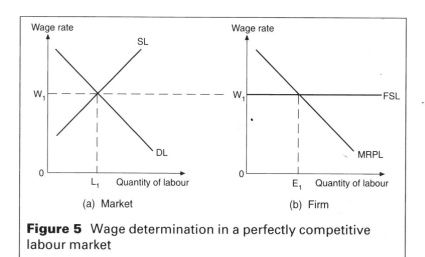

Figure 5 Wage determination in a perfectly competitive labour market

perfectly competitive then each firm is one of many hirers of labour and must pay the competitive labour market wage.

Monopsony

The monopsony model of the labour market assumes that there are a large number of employees, but one dominant employer whose employment decisions directly affect the wage rate. The dominant employer is called a **monopsonist**. This situation is most likely to occur in circumstances where a large single plant such as a steel mill, coalmine or textile factory is the major employer within a local labour market and where there are problems of labour mobility. *When labour is mobile the number of potential employers increases and the labour market ceases to be monopsonistic.*

Figure 6 illustrates the case of the profit maximizing monopsonist. The labour market demand curve (DL) shows the firm's marginal revenue product of labour at each level of employment. The labour market supply curve (SL) shows the quantity of labour supplied at each wage rate. In order to attract an extra unit of labour the firm must offer a higher wage rate to all units of labour employed. Consequently, the marginal cost of employing an additional unit of labour (MCL) will be greater than the wage rate at each level of employment.

For example, if a monopsonist employing 100 workers at a wage rate of £250 per week increases the wage rate to £252 per week to attract an additional employee, the marginal cost of labour will be £252 + (100 × £2) = £452.

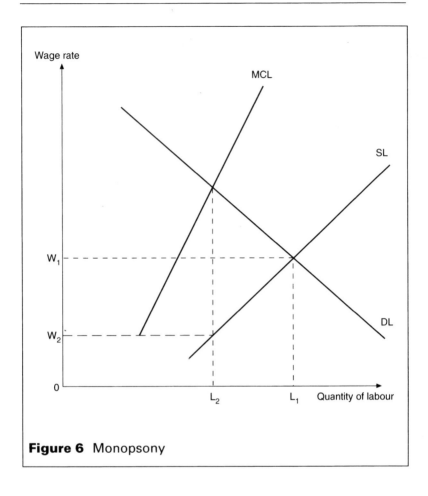

Figure 6 Monopsony

The quantity of labour employed will be increased as long as the marginal revenue product of labour exceeds the marginal cost. In Figure 6, the quantity of labour employed by the profit maximizing monopsonist will be L_2 and the wage rate will be W_2. This contrasts with a competitive labour market with the same labour market supply and demand curves, which would give an equilibrium of L_1 and W_1. *The monopsonist is able to exploit the labour market by paying a wage rate which is less than the marginal revenue product of labour.*

Components of wage rates

The wage rate received by an employee can be divided into two components, called **economic rent** and **transfer earnings**. *Transfer earnings are the minimum payment necessary to keep a factor of production in its pre-*

sent use and discourage it from moving to an alternative employment. Economic rent is any payment in excess of transfer earnings. For most workers, wages will include both components, but in extreme cases wages will be entirely economic rent or transfer earnings.

The three possible cases are illustrated in Figures 7 (a), (b) and (c). Each diagram shows the labour market supply and demand curves (SL and DL respectively), and the equilibrium wage (W_1) and number of workers employed (L_1).

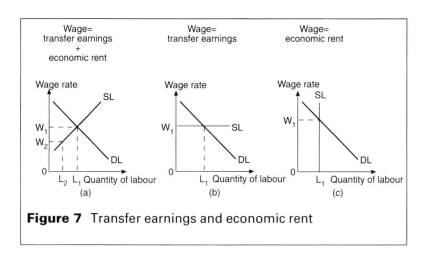

Figure 7 Transfer earnings and economic rent

At each wage rate the marginal worker is just prepared to remain in that employment but would transfer out if wages fell. For example, in Figure 7(a) the wage rate of W_2 gives a supply of labour equal to L_2. The wage rate, W_2, is the marginal worker's supply price or transfer earnings, the minimum payment required to keep the worker in that employment. As the wage rate is increased, additional workers, with higher transfer earnings, will enter the occupation thereby increasing the labour market supply. At the equilibrium wage rate W_1, the supply of labour is L_1 and all of the income of the marginal worker is transfer earnings. For all other employees the wage rate will be above their transfer earnings and they consequently earn some economic rent.

Suppose a male student who works part-time in a supermarket is paid £3.75 per hour. In his next-best alternative employment he could earn £3 per hour. He would transfer to the alternative employment if the supermarket hourly wage rate was cut below £3. Thus his transfer-earnings are £3 per hour and he receives 75 pence per hour economic rent.

In Figure 7(b), the labour market supply curve is perfectly wage elastic at the equilibrium wage rate. In this case the wages paid consist entirely of transfer earnings.

In Figure 7(c), the labour market supply curve is completely wage inelastic. Whatever the wage rate the supply of labour is fixed at L_1. In this case the wage paid consists entirely of economic rent and depends on the demand for labour.

A substantial part of the income earned by individuals with specialized talents that are in short supply will be economic rent. For example, payments to personalities with skills that are difficult to replicate in sports and entertainment will include a high proportion of economic rent.

TOP SPORTS EARNINGS
1993–94

Nigel Mansell	£9.0 m
Lennox Lewis	£5.2 m
Chris Eubank	£3.4 m
Nick Faldo	£2.4 m
David Platt	£2.2 m
Gary Lineker	£1.5 m
Stephen Hendry	£1.4 m
Colin Montgomerie	£1.4 m
Nigel Benn	£1.2 m

Wage differentials

Wage differentials can be observed in all labour markets. The following are examples of average hourly earnings paid to full-time employees in 1994:

- Men working in professional occupations received £13.23 and women £12.07. Male clerical and secretarial staff received £6.68 and women £6.02. Male plant and machine operators received £6.25 and women £4.67.

- *Non-manual* male workers in the banking, finance, insurance and business services sector received £13.39 and women £7.73. Non-manual male workers in the distribution, hotels and catering sector received £8.00 and women £5.32.
- Male *manual* workers in the banking, finance, insurance and business services sector received £5.66 and women £5.01. Male manual workers in the distribution, hotels and catering sector received £5.32 and women £3.99.

The reasons why wages differ can be examined under five headings.

1. Labour market imperfections

Labour market imperfections can exist on the demand side, the supply side, or both. As the earlier analysis demonstrates, wages will be lower when the employer is a monopsonist. On the supply side, trade unions are the most likely source of labour market imperfections. By threatening a strike or controlling the supply of labour it may be possible for a trade union to force up the wage rate at the cost of lower levels of employment. When the labour market includes a combination of trade union control and monopsony the wage rate and the level of employment will depend on the bargaining power of the two parties. Trade union activity will be examined in more detail in the next chapter.

Where there is imperfect information in the labour market, employees may not be well-informed about the availability of work at different wage rates. Consequently, time will be spent looking for a job offering an acceptable wage rate. This process will involve costs, including forgone wages, when low-paid jobs are rejected in favour of looking for something better. **Search theory** tells us that the acceptable wage will be lower the longer the employee takes searching for a job.

2. Education and training

Employees who are prepared to invest in vocational education and training make themselves more productive and consequently achieve higher wage rates than unskilled labour. The process of acquiring skills is called **human capital investment**. In particular, workers who have developed skills that are in short supply will have the opportunity of commanding high wages. Many professional occupations require a high level of skill involving several years of full-time higher education in university or college, whilst others will require intermediate qualifications. The consequence for wage rates is illustrated in Figure 8.

19

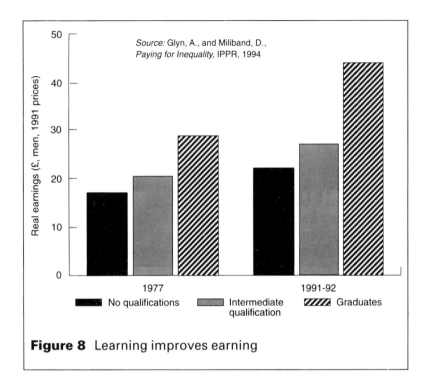

Figure 8 Learning improves earning

What is quite clear in the labour markets of the modern industrial economy is that the demand for skilled labour continues to rise whilst the employment opportunities of the unskilled continue to fall (see Chapter 6). This is the result of technical change where new technology replaces the unskilled worker and skilled workers are demanded to develop and implement the new technology.

Figure 9 illustrates the case of two labour markets where initially the equilibrium wage rates are WS_1 in the skilled market and WU_1 in the unskilled market. A change in technology increases the demand for skilled labour from DS_1 to DS_2 and reduces the demand for unskilled labour from DU_1 to DU_2. The result, in the short run, is a reduction in the employment of unskilled labour from LU_1 to LU_2, an increase in the employment of skilled labour from LS_1 to LS_2, and a widening gap between skilled and unskilled wages, now WS_2 and WU_2 respectively. In the long run, the wage differential should encourage more employees to acquire marketable skills, so reducing the supply of unskilled labour from SU_1 to SU_2 and increasing the supply of skilled labour from SS_1 to SS_2. This will give a long-run adjustment of skilled and unskilled wages to WS_3 and WU_3 respectively.

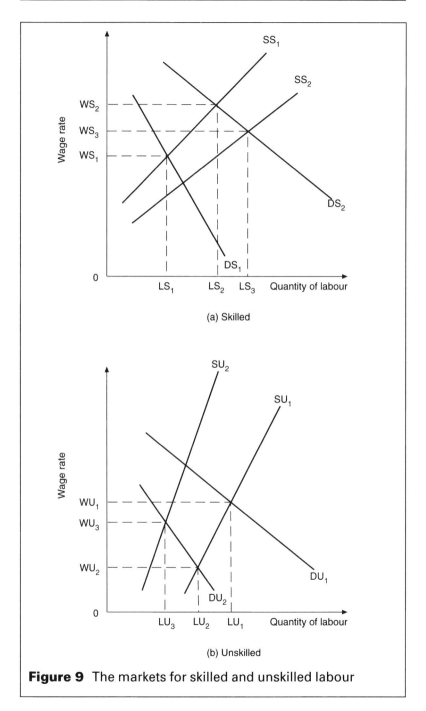

Figure 9 The markets for skilled and unskilled labour

TECHNOLOGY AND UNEMPLOYMENT

Since the beginning of the industrial revolution people have predicted that machines would destroy jobs. In the early 19th century the Luddites responded by destroying the looms and jennies that threatened their livelihood. Marx said that, by investing in machinery, factory owners would create a vast army of unemployed. And in the late 1940s Norbert Weiner, a pioneer of computing, forecast that this new technology would destroy enough jobs to make the depression of the 1930s look like a picnic.

Fear of what machines will do to men at work waxes and wanes. Right now, the fear is growing strongly. Typical of the new wave of pessimistic forecasts is a book, *The End of Work* (G. P. Putnam's Sons), by Jeremy Rifkin, an American technophobe whose previous target was the biotechnology industry. Within the next century, he predicts, the world's rich economies will have virtually no need of workers. Predictions such as this reinforce a growing fear in the middle classes that technology, having eliminated much of the work previously done by manual workers, is about to cut a swathe through white-collar ranks as well.

Are such fears justified? In one way, yes. Millions of jobs have indeed been destroyed by technology. A decade ago, the words you are now reading would have reached you from two sets of hands: those of a journalist and those of a typesetter. Thanks to computers, the typesetter no longer has a job. But cheer up–a bit anyway. Although the typesetter no longer has *that* job, he may well have a different one. John Kennedy put it well in the 1960s: "If men have the talent to invent new machines that put men out of work, they have the talent to put those men back to work". That is as true now as it was then, and earlier.

In the past 200 years millions of manual workers have been replaced by machines. Over the same period, the number of jobs has grown almost continuously, as have the real incomes of most people in the industrial world. Furthermore, this growth and enrichment have come about not in spite of technological change but because of it.

The idea that technology is capable of creating more jobs than it destroys, and will do so again, would not surprise an economist.

A new machine helps you make more stuff with fewer people. But the assumption that this results in fewer jobs rather than more output (and hence more goods and more job-stimulating demand, in a beautifully virtuous circle) is based on an economic fallacy known as the "lump of labour": the notion that there is only a fixed amount of output (and hence work) to go round. This is clearly wrong. Technology creates new demand, either by increasing productivity and hence real incomes, or by creating new goods.

Source: *The Economist*, 11 Feb. 1995

Read the clipping from the *Times*.

Poor education frustrates help plan on jobs

The government's attempts to regenerate economically depressed areas of Britain are being thwarted by low standards of education and training, the minister responsible for regional development claimed yesterday.

Tim Eggar told MPs on the Trade and Industry Select Committee that although the government's regional aid was helping to reduce levels of unemployment, its effectiveness was limited by poor levels of training and basic educational skills. Some parts of the country "do suffer very low educational aspirations both by teachers and parents," he said. There was a willingness to accept levels of education "no longer appropriate to a modern and dynamic industrial society".

Britain still had a lot to make up on its competitors in the level of technical skills of its workforce before it could bring economic revival to the relatively poor regions of the north and west of Britain, he said.

The government currently spends between £100 and £150 million a year on industrial grants for the English regions, down from £250 million to £300 million in the late 1980s. Mr Eggar gave warning that much of the assistance could be wasted unless technical skills were raised.

The Times, 19 January 1995

3. Working conditions

There are many characteristics of a job which will influence the quantity of labour supplied at each wage rate. Jobs that are generally less attractive must pay a **compensating wage differential**. Where either the nature of the work to be undertaken, or the working conditions, are undesirable the market supply of labour will be reduced and it will be necessary to offer higher wages in order to attract the desired quantity of labour supply. Similarly, occupations which involve working unsociable hours command higher wages than comparable occupations undertaken during normal working hours. In occupations where there is a high degree of risk of injury or death, employees will be reluctant to take on the risk without an appropriate compensating differential built into the wage rate. In other circumstances, the occupation may involve a number of **non-monetary benefits**. For example, long holidays with pay, a shorter working week, pleasant working conditions or the opportunity to travel will increase the market supply of labour, resulting in a correspondingly lower equilibrium wage rate.

4. Regional variations

Regional differences in labour supply and demand will cause variations in wage rates. Where these exist in comparable labour markets, we might expect to see employers and employees transferring from one region to another. Whilst employees will be attracted to regions where wages are relatively high, employers will have an incentive to do the opposite. The resulting adjustments to labour market supply and demand will eventually bring equality to wage rates in comparable labour markets in different regions. National negotiations of wage rates will also bring a degree of equality to occupational wage levels in different localities. Figure 10, which shows average gross hourly earnings for five major occupational groups in the south-east and north-east of England and in Scotland, illustrates the similarity between occupational wages in different regions.

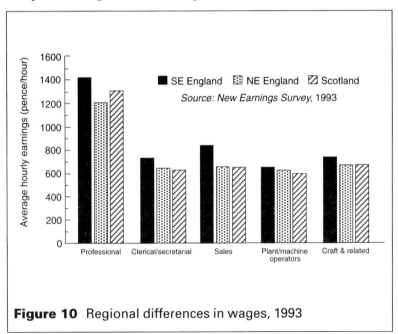

Figure 10 Regional differences in wages, 1993

5. Discrimination

Wage discrimination occurs when, for reasons of age, sex or race, employees of equal proficiency are paid different wage rates by an employer for the same work. Empirical studies in the UK suggest that on average non-white males earn 17 per cent less than white males, whilst women earn over 20 per cent less than men. In both cases there are two main explanations, each of which accounts for approximately half of the difference.

- First, differences in education, productivity and training result in women and non-white males working predominantly in low-paid industries and occupations and being under-represented in higher-paid jobs.
- Secondly, even when education and experience are comparable, wage discrimination has resulted in women and non-white men being paid less for doing the same work as white men. Furthermore, **employment discrimination** in the form of a *glass ceiling* – an invisible block to promotion – has restricted access to better paid jobs.

Some improvement in the situation has taken place as a result of the introduction of three statutes:

- the 1970 Equal Pay Act
- the 1975 Sex Discrimination Act
- the 1976 Race Relations Act.

It is estimated that prior to the introduction of the Equal Pay Act women's average hourly earnings were less than two-thirds those of men. Figure 11 shows how the average hourly earnings of men and women employees have changed over 20 years.

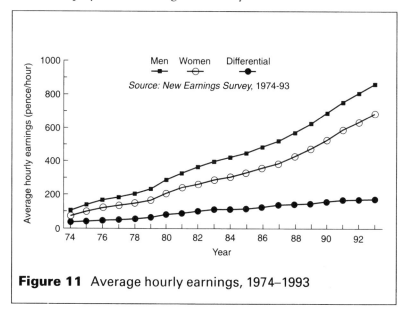

Figure 11 Average hourly earnings, 1974–1993

Conclusion

There are clearly a number of explanations for the diversity of wage rates in the UK economy, but the most important is differences in the supply and demand for labour. Moreover, not all labour markets are perfect, and imperfections exist on both the supply and demand sides of such markets. Consequently, wages do not always reflect the value of labour's marginal product.

KEY WORDS

Monopsonist	Human capital investment
Economic rent	Compensating wage
Transfer earnings	differential
Search theory	Non-monetary benefits

Reading list

Beardshaw, J., Chapter 21 in *Economics – A Student' s Guide*, 3rd edn, Pitman, 1992.

Paisley, R., and Quillfeldt, J., Unit 23 in *Economics Investigated*, vol. 2, Collins Educational, 1992.

Whynes, D., Chapter 4 in *Welfare State Economics*, Heinemann Educational, 1992.

Essay topics

1. (a) What determines the demand for labour in a given industry? [30 marks]
   (b) Examine the factors that determine the earnings of each of the following groups of people: (i) nurses, (ii) divers working on North Sea oil rigs, and (iii) law court judges. [70 marks]
   [University of London Examinations and Assessment Council 1992]
2. (a) Outline how the marginal revenue productivity theory suggests that the level of wages in an industry is determined. [13 marks]
   (b) How realistic do you consider this explanation to be? [12 marks]
   [University of Cambridge Local Examinations Syndicate 1993])
3. (a) Why are there differences in the wage rates paid to people in different occupations? [12 marks]
   (b) Discuss the view that high wages will inevitably result in lower levels of employment. [13 marks]
   [Associated Examining Board 1993]

Data Response Question 2

The demand for labour
This task is based on a question in a new-syllabus specimen paper from the University of Cambridge Local Examinations Syndicate. Study Figures A and B (both taken from *Employment Gazette*, April 1993) and Table A (from *New Earnings Survey*, November 1993), before tackling the questions that follow.

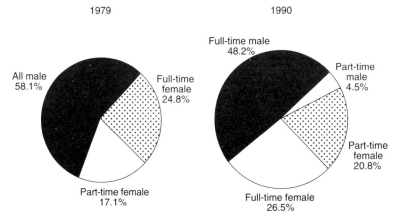

Figure A Composition of employees by sex and full-time/part-time status

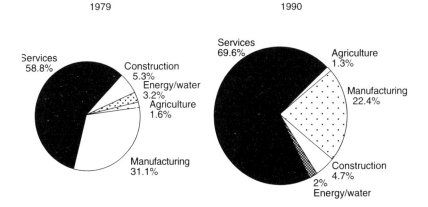

Figure B Composition of employees by industrial sector

Table A Average gross weekly earnings for full-time employees by occupational group, April 1993 (including those whose pay was affected by absence)

	Managers and administrators	Receptionists	Nurses	Police sergeant and below
Male	£498.10	£230.20	£318.20	£430.70
Female	£336.30	£172.70	£293.10	£378.00

	Textile & tannery process operatives	Road transport operatives	Primary & nursey school teachers	Secondary school teachers
Male	£240.90	£254.70	£428.20	£442.10
Female	£165.60	£190.80	£367.40	£388.00

1. (a) How has the labour force changed, (i) by sex and (ii) by full-time/part-time status, between 1979 and 1990? [2 marks]
   (b) Suggest *two* likely reasons for changes you have identified. [4 marks]
2. (a) In Figure B, what evidence is there of deindustrialization? [2 marks]
   (b) State one other way in which deindustrialization affects the demand for labour. [1 mark]
3. (a) Which occupations have (i) the largest and (ii) the smallest difference between average weekly earnings paid to males and females? [2 marks]
   (b) Excluding sex discrimination, explain *two* reasons why males earn more than females in all of the occupations shown in Table A. [4 marks]
4. Discuss how UK government policy might seek to equalize the average weekly earnings of male and female full-time employees. [5 marks]

Chapter Three

Trade unions

'A trade union, as we understand the term, is a continuous association of wage-earners for the purpose of maintaining or improving the conditions of their working lives.'
Sidney and Beatrice Webb

In the absence of trade unions individual employees are obliged to negotiate their own contracts with employers. Employers are generally in a significantly more powerful bargaining position than individual employees, especially in times of widespread unemployment. The formation of trade unions has been the result. Unions try to establish negotiating rights over their members' wages and conditions of employment and to limit managerial authority over labour after its hire. In effect, the activities of trade unions are designed to limit the power of employers by replacing unilateral decisions with agreed rules and procedures. Trade union membership increased to more than half of the workforce during the 1970s but has subsequently declined to just over a third.

The functions of unions

Historically, the main function of trade unions has been to engage in **collective bargaining**. This term is used to describe *the process by which rates of pay and other conditions of employment are negotiated by employers and representatives of their employees.* It is collective because employees associate together, normally in trade unions, to bargain with their employers. The process is referred to as bargaining because each side is able to bring pressure to bear on the other, such as a strike or lockout.

Unions may also seek to achieve particular objectives through **political action**. Such action has, at certain times, resulted in legislation to regulate conditions of employment and thus removed some issues from the scope of collective bargaining – at least with regard to setting minimum standards. The employment of young persons, the reasons justifying dismissal, maternity leave rights and health and safety procedures are all examples of such matters. A number of unions are affiliated to the Labour party and this reflects a recognition that they need to engage in political as well as industrial action to further the interests of their members. The Labour party's consultations with its members over proposed changes to Clause Four of its constitution included seeking the views of affiliated unions.

Other unions rely on the Trades Union Congress to make representations to the government and to persuade it to introduce desired social and employment legislation.

Effects of trade unions on wages and employment

Trade unions may be able to raise wages in a firm or industry above the rate that would have prevailed in their absence, but this will have implications for the level of employment in that firm or industry.

If a union is able to negotiate a wage rate greater than the equilibrium level – perhaps by persuading workers to take or to threaten to take strike action – then in a competitive labour market the level of employment will fall.

This is illustrated in Figure 12 in which the labour market supply curve is initially SL_1 and the labour market demand curve is DL. In the absence of a trade union, the equilibrium wage rate is W_1 and the equilibrium level of employment is L_1. If the trade union is able to force the firm to pay a wage rate of W_2, when the labour market supply curve remains at SL_1, the level of employment will fall to L_2 and the supply of labour will rise to L_3. This will give an excess labour supply of $L_3 - L_2$.

If the union is powerful enough to insist that the equilibrium level of employment L_1 is maintained, the firm would be overstaffed, less competitive and in danger of going out of business.

Another way in which a trade union may be able to raise wages is to restrict the supply of labour. This might be accomplished by controlling employee training or selection arrangements in some way, or by limiting access to jobs to those belonging to the union – that is by imposing a **closed shop**. The effect of such restrictions would be to reduce the supply of labour at each wage rate so that the labour market supply curve shifts to the left.

This is shown in Figure 12 with a move from SL_1 to SL_2, the consequence of which is a rise in the wage rate to W_2 and a fall in the level of employment to L_2. In a competitive labour market, therefore, the raising of wages by trade union activity leads to a fall in the level of employment.

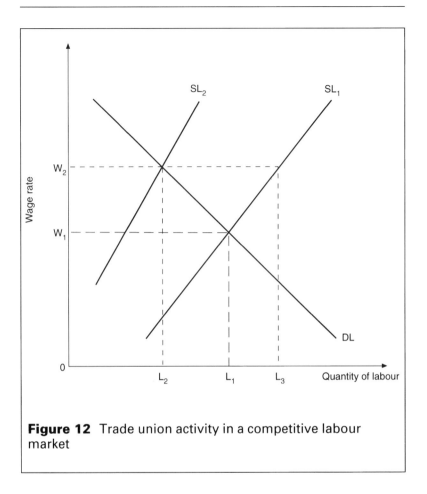

Figure 12 Trade union activity in a competitive labour market

Empirical studies which have investigated the effect of trade unions on wage levels have shown that the wages of union members tend to be higher than those of equivalent non-union employees. This **union mark-up** varies between occupations and is particularly significant in closed-shop situations. It has been suggested that the average union mark-up in the early 1980s was 10 per cent or a little less, after which it declined somewhat.

Empirical evidence on the employment consequences of trade union activity is somewhat scanty. One study relating to the period 1980–84 concluded that trade unions had a negative impact on the growth of employment in the private sector of approximately three percentage points. In other words, unionized workplaces lost 3 per cent more jobs, or gained 3 per cent fewer jobs, each year than non-union workplaces. It has been suggested, however, that the slower employment growth in unionized plants between 1980 and 1984 may have been due to an increase in productivity growth as a result of changes in working practices. The giving up by trade unions, at a time of recession, of some of the restrictions on the use of labour they had previously been able to impose could largely explain the disproportionate decline in employment in unionized establishments.

Effects of trade unions on productivity

The overall effect of trade unions on labour productivity is a much debated matter. Different attitudes towards flexibility in the use of labour and technological change in different workplaces will have different consequences for productivity, even if the degree of unionization is similar. The presence of trade unions may increase productivity if the unions support management efforts to reduce inefficiency and if cooperation between employees and managers is encouraged. Higher productivity may also occur when trade union activity keeps managers aware of, and alive to, what is happening at the workplace.

It has been argued that unions can help to raise productivity levels by giving employees a 'collective voice' in the company, thereby improving communications and reducing labour turnover and waste. If, however, trade unions are uncooperative as far as technological or organisational change is concerned, if there are frequent disputes between employees and managers, or if unions are able to maintain excessive manning levels or restrictive work rules, productivity is likely to be adversely affected.

The efficient use of labour in much of British industry was hindered for many years by **overstaffing** ('overmanning') and the existence of working practices such as **demarcation**.

- *Overstaffing* occurs when trade unions can persuade an employing organization to employ more workers at the prevailing wage rate than it would prefer to hire. Industries that have suffered from overstaffing include the railways, motor car manufacturing and printing.
- *Demarcation* is an attempt to maintain the demand for a certain type of labour. Traditionally, within a British factory different unions reserved areas of work for their own members. This restricted management's deployment of its labour force, sometimes very considerably. Industries in which demarcation was a particular problem included steel and shipbuilding.

The growth of trade union power

By the late 1970s there was a growing public conviction that trade unions in the UK had become too powerful. They were criticized over the frequency of strikes, the existence of overstaffing and restrictive working practices, and for causing higher unemployment by pushing wages above market-clearing levels. The strengthening position of the unions during the 1970s had been the result of a number of factors, including favourable legislation, a rapid growth of union membership and the expansion of the closed shop.

- Legislation introduced by the Labour government between 1974 and 1979 added to the powers of unions. The major employment statute during this period was the Employment Protection Act of 1975, which introduced a number of positive legal rights for trade unions and individual employees.
- Trade union membership grew rapidly during the 1970s, both in absolute and relative terms. As Figure 13 shows, the membership of unions rose by more than three million between 1968 and 1979 (an increase of 30 per cent). **Union density**, that is the proportion of the workforce who are union members, also went up from 44 per cent to 54.5 per cent.
- Between the early 1960s and the late 1970s the number of employees affected by closed shop agreements increased from 3.75 million to over 5 million.

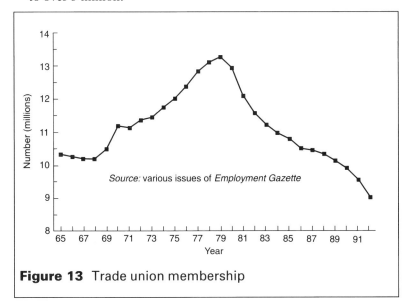

Figure 13 Trade union membership

Controlling the unions

Since 1979 successive Conservative governments have introduced legislation to reduce the power of trade unions in order to make labour markets more responsive to changing economic conditions. A series of statutes has placed restrictions on trade union activity, particularly in relation to strikes and the closed shop. The legislation, however, has also been concerned with democracy in trade unions and the recognition of unions by employers.

- The Employment Act of 1980 outlawed **secondary picketing** by restricting lawful picketing to a person's own workplace. Another Employment Act in 1990 made all forms of secondary action by union members unlawful.
- The legal definition of a trade dispute was narrowed in 1982 in an attempt to prevent political strikes and inter-union disputes. A trade dispute must wholly or mainly relate to employment matters and must be between workers and their employer.
- The Trade Union Act of 1984 introduced the requirement of a **pre-strike ballot** for unions. If a strike is called by a union without the support of the majority of the participants, voting in a secret ballot, the employer concerned can sue the union. Since 1993 unions have also had to give at least seven days' notice of strikes.
- The view was taken that closed shops were an infringement of the freedom of individuals and caused economic damage by raising labour costs and fostering inefficient ways of working. Statutory support for them was, therefore, gradually removed.
- It was claimed that some unions were undemocractic and controlled by unrepresentative minorities. The Trade Union Act of 1984 required the members of the main executive committee of a trade union to be elected by a secret ballot of all the union's members at least once every five years.
- Legislation supporting the recognition of trade unions for bargaining purposes by employers, enacted in 1975 by a Labour government, was repealed in 1980.

The impact of the legislation

As Table 2 shows, the number of stoppages and working days lost due to industrial disputes were both much lower in the 1980s, especially during the second half of the decade, than they had been during the 1970s. Moreover, in the early 1990s strike activity continued to decline. The main reasons for the decline in strike activity since 1979, however, appear to have been economic. Rising unemployment between 1979 and 1986, and again between 1989 and 1993, reduced the willingness of employees to take strike action. This was accompanied by a significant restructuring of the economy, with a decline in strongly unionized and more strike-prone traditional industries and a growth in poorly unionized and less strike-prone service industries.

Table 2 Stoppages of work due to industrial disputes in the UK, 1965–93

Years	Average number of stoppages per year	Average number of working days lost per year
1965–69	2 380	3 929 000
1970–74	2 885	14 077 000
1975–79	2 310	11 663 000
1980–84	1 351	10 486 000
1985–89	881	3 940 000
1990–93	355	960 000

Source: Calculated from annual data in various issues of *Employment Gazette*

Nevertheless, changes in the law do seem to have had an influence on strike activity. The narrowing of the definition of a trade dispute, the outlawing of secondary picketing and of other forms of secondary action have all had some impact, but *there is little doubt that the most important legislative change has been the pre-strike ballot requirement introduced in 1984.* Since then ballots have become an increasingly common feature of the negotiating process with union members generally coming to regard them as an essential precursor to strike action. Indeed, ballots have sometimes been used to put pressure on an employer to make a better offer, which is then accepted. So the growing use of ballots has helped to reduce the number of strikes, not least because a clear majority in favour of strike action often leads employers to improve their offer and thus to a peaceful settlement.

The legislation dealing with the closed shop has helped to reduce its coverage significantly, although in the early 1980s the number of employees in closed shops fell mainly because of a contraction of employment in industries and companies where union membership was compulsory. A five-year review ballot rule for the maintenance of existing closed shops, introduced in 1982, proved to be highly significant. Relatively few ballots were held and a number of large employers terminated their closed shop agreements with trade unions or gave a commitment that no employees would lose their jobs simply because they declined to be union members. However, despite dismissal for non-membership of a union being made automatically unfair in 1988, a considerable number of closed shops continued to operate on an informal basis and a survey in 1989 suggested that the total number of employees in closed shops was still of the order of 2.5 million. The legislation has put an end to formal agreements enforcing the closed shop, but in many workplaces with a long closed shop tradition informal pressures to ensure that employees belong to a trade union doubtless remain.

Government hostility towards trade unions has rubbed off on many employers and this has resulted in companies often refusing to recognize unions on new (greenfield) employment sites. A problem unions face, therefore, is that when older unionized workplaces close down they are typically replaced by non-union workplaces in different industries. This has reinforced the decline in the membership of trade unions, which fell to little more than nine million in 1992 (see Figure 13). Britain's trade unions are in a very much weaker position today than they were in the late 1970s.

KEY WORDS

Collective bargaining	Demarcation
Political action	Union density
Closed shop	Secondary picketing
Union mark-up	Pre-strike ballot
Overstaffing	

Reading list

Healey, N., *Supply Side Economics*, 3rd edn, Heinemann Educational, 1996.

Paterson, I. and Simpson, L., 'The economics of trade union power', in Healey, N., *Britain's Economic Miracle: Myth or Reality?*, Routledge, 1993.

Smith, D., Chapter 5 in *Mrs. Thatcher's Economics: Her Legacy*, 2nd edn, Heinemann Educational, 1992.

Essay topics

1. Discuss whether trade unions can increase the real incomes of their members and the level of employment in the industries in which they operate. [25 marks]
   [Associated Examining Board 1992]

2. Do you agree that the higher wages paid in some occupations occur solely because some trade unionists have a stronger bargaining position than others? [25 marks]
[University of Cambridge Local Examinations Syndicate 1992]

3. 'If trade unions increase their members' wages, they will also cause unemployment.' Explain, and evaluate, this statement. [25 marks]
[Welsh Joint Education Committee 1993]

4. (a) Explain how marginal revenue productivity theory can be used to analyse the equilibrium level of wages and employment in an industry where there is no trade union. [15 marks]
(b) Discuss the possible effect on this equlibrium of the introduction of trade union wage bargaining. [10 marks]
[University of Cambridge Local Examinations Syndicate 1994]

Data Response Question 3

Trade unions in Britain

This task is based on a question set by the Oxford & Cambridge Schools Examination Board in 1992. Study Table A and then answer the questions.

Table A

	Number of unions at end of year	Total union membership (thousands)	Number of industrial stoppages	Working days lost in industrial stoppages (thousands)
1979	453	13 289	2 125	29 474
1980	438	12 947	1 348	11 964
1981	414	12 106	1 344	4 266
1982	408	11 593	1 538	5 313
1983	394	11 236	1 364	3 754
1984	375	10 994	1 221	27 135
1985	370	10 821	903	6 402
1986	335	10 539	1 074	1 920
1987	330	10 475	1 016	3 546
1988	315	10 376	781	3 702
1989	309	10 158	701	4 128
1990	301 (est)	9 940 (est)	630	1 903

Source: *Employment Gazette*, June and July 1991

1. Account for the decline in the number of unions and in total union membership between 1979 and 1990. [9 marks]
2. Account for the decline in industrial stoppages and in working days lost between 1979 and 1990. [9 marks]
3. Can it be concluded that trade union power is now no longer of importance? [7 marks]

Chapter Four
Minimum wages

'Wage-fixing laws usually hurt the people they want to help.'
Editorial in *The Economist*

The concept of **low pay** is inevitably a subjective one and various definitions have been suggested. They tend to relate low pay to average pay in some way, so that low pay is usually defined in relative terms – less than two-thirds of average earnings, for instance. But whatever definition of low pay is adopted, more people are now low-paid than they were in 1979.

Low pay in the UK has been and remains one of the causes of poverty. In November 1994 the Low Pay Unit, an independent research organization, estimated that 37 per cent of full-time employees were receiving less than 68 per cent of average earnings, the Council of Europe's so-called 'decency threshold'.

- However, many low-paid workers do not live in low-income households and are not, therefore, in family poverty.
- In any case, poverty in families depends on the number of dependants as well as wage rates.
- Moreover, many people in poverty do not have a job and so would not benefit from higher wage rates.
- Nevertheless, raising the earnings of those in low-paid employment would help to reduce the number of families in poverty, and one way of bringing this about would be to introduce a **national minimum wage.**

More importantly perhaps, a minimum wage would give protection to those employees – many of them women and part-time workers – whose weak position in the labour market enables employers to take advantage of them by paying low wages. Such employees often have domestic responsibilities which limit their availability for work and make them take whatever jobs they can get. Employers rarely offer them jobs for which much skill is required and consequently they receive little training, which limits their chances of obtaining other employment or promotion.

The case against a national minimum wage is that it would result in an increase in labour costs and therefore in job losses, although the employment impact would also depend on the extent to which firms could pass on additional costs to consumers in the form of higher prices.

Two Cambridge economists, Peter Brosnan and Frank Wilkinson, have forecast the impact on direct labour costs of introducing a national minimum wage in the UK. Their estimates were that a minimum wage set at half average earnings would increase direct labour costs by 0.9 per cent and that a minimum wage set at two-thirds of average earnings would cause direct labour costs to rise by some 3.6 per cent. There were, however, considerable variations between industries and therefore they proposed that any national minimum wage should initially be set at half average earnings and be linked with other policies designed to encourage job creation.

Effects of minimum wages on employment

The employment effects of introducing a minimum wage must be examined carefully. Figure 14 assumes a perfectly competitive labour market, where SL is the labour market supply curve for low-paid occupations and DL is the corresponding labour market demand curve. The labour market for low-paid occupations is in equilibrium when the wage rate is equal to W_1 and the level of employment is L_1. If a national minimum wage rate of W_2 were to be introduced, the demand for labour would fall from L_1 to L_2 while the supply of labour would rise from L_1 to L_3. Involuntary unemployment equal to $L_3 - L_2$ would be the result. The effect of the minimum wage on employment will be greater the more elastic is the labour market demand curve (DL).

Wages and the productivity of labour

There is a need for caution when drawing policy conclusions on the basis of the above analysis. Implicit in the argument is an assumption that changes in the wage rate do not affect the productivity of labour. However, it is possible that the increase in wages resulting from the introduction of a minimum wage could increase labour productivity and, if that happens, the demand curve for labour would shift to the right and reduce the negative effect of higher wages on employment levels.

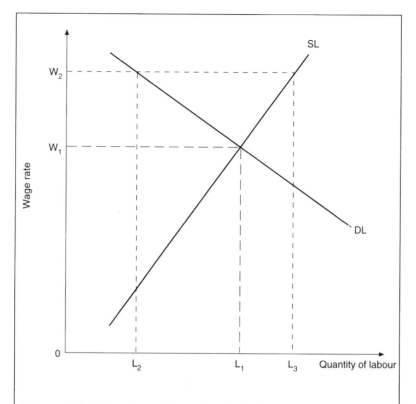

Figure 14 The effect of a national minimum wage on low-paid occupations

There are two reasons why an increase in wages could lead to an increase in labour productivity.

- The first is called the **efficiency wage effect,** which is often experienced in poor countries when an increase in wages improves worker nutrition and health, making the labour force more productive. In developed nations employers may find that higher wages improve the morale of their employees and encourage them to work harder and up to their full capabilities.
- Secondly, it is possible that a wage increase may improve the efficiency of management. Firms that rely on cheap labour can often survive despite inefficiencies in the production process and the use of outdated technology. When confronted with the need to pay a minimum wage, management may be shocked into using labour

more productively in order to compete. Managerial reactions to higher wage rates which result in increased labour productivity are called **shock effects**.

Empirical studies of minimum wages

A study undertaken by Stephen Bazen of the University of Kent, published in 1990, examined the consequences for UK employment of introducing a national minimum wage at half and two-thirds of male median earnings. He estimated that the two levels of minimum wage would increase average earnings by 2 per cent and 7 per cent respectively. The corresponding reductions in employment were 250 000 and 885 000.

Minimum-wage legislation at federal and state level has existed in the USA for many years, thus enabling researchers to investigate its actual impact. Some recent empirical studies suggest that labour market imperfections are such that the wage rates of low-paid workers can be raised to some extent at least without harmful effects on employment levels (see the extract from the *Guardian*).

The empirical evidence suggests that the economic impact of minimum wages is much less clear-cut than is often supposed. The extent of any unemployment effect depends on:

- the level of the minimum wage
- the elasticities of demand and supply of labour in the low-wage sectors of the economy
- the size of any efficiency wage or shock effects.

Minimum wages in the UK

Although a national minimum wage has never been introduced in Britain, for many years arrangements existed to fix legal minimum wages in specific industries.

Initially, minimum wages were fixed by various **trade boards** set up under legislation enacted in 1909 and 1918. The legislation was the result of widespread public concern about the practice that existed in a number of industries of forcing people to work very hard for little pay. The problem of 'sweated labour', as it became known, was the subject of a number of enquiries, including one by the House of Lords, and it was eventually decided to allow minimum wage rates to be fixed in industries where wage rates were exceptionally low.

In 1945 the trade boards were replaced by **wages councils**. The main areas of employment covered by wages councils were retail distribu-

US findings defy logic that minimum wage costs jobs

EDWARD BALLS

Economists, the cliché runs, only ever agree to disagree. But there has been at least one rule that most have tended to assert – minimum wages cost jobs.

Yet recent US evidence suggests that the opposite is true – an increase in the US minimum wage to a tolerable level does not appear to have cost jobs. If anything, it has marginally increased employment.

David Card, of Princeton University, examined the effect of the increase in the federal minimum wage from $3.35 to $3.80 (£2.53) an hour in 1990. He compared its impact on states with differing proportions of low-wage workers on the assumption that if the increase in the national minimum wage reduced low-wage employment, then total employment should fall faster in low-wage states.

But he found no significant differences in employment growth in the following year. If anything, employment grew faster in low-wage states.

The US evidence is overwhelming and the reason is that labour markets do not operate like the markets for apples or beans.

The classic "commonsense" view depends, in fact, on highly restrictive assumptions about labour markets; assuming that employers can hire as many of the kinds of workers they need and that employees have a detailed knowledge of jobs and wages.

But these assumptions are almost never met. Even when the economy is booming, both companies and individuals have to spend time searching for each other. And workers with the same skills and experiences often earn very different wages.

This "commonsense" view is particularly inappropriate in low-wage, low-skill, service sector industries where turnover is rapid, employment local and workers young or inexperienced.

Employers find here that they can make extra profits paying below-market wages to their employees but are deterred from expansion because advertising for workers at the new market rate would mean a wage increase for the whole workforce. Setting a minimum wage closer to the market wage for unskilled workers bites into these excess profits but the result seems to be to encourage companies to hire more people to make up some of the lost profit.

Of course, raising minimum wages too far will eventually bite into employment. The special nature of low-wage labour markets means raising minimum wages to a tolerable level to prevent exploitation does not appear to cost jobs but raising minimum wages above the market rate does.

The Guardian, 2 May 1994

tion and the hotel, catering and clothing industries. However, by the mid-1980s the government took the view that wages councils had contributed to the rise in unemployment by fixing wages above the level at which people, especially the young, would be prepared to work. Furthermore the government argued that minimum wages were inconsistent with the need for **flexible pay determination**. There were 26 wages councils in existence, setting legal minimum wage rates for some 2.5 million employees, when the system was eventually brought to an end in 1993.

Explaining why the time had come to abolish all the wages councils, the Secretary of State for Employment claimed that 80 per cent of those employed in wages-council industries lived in households with at least one other source of income. The government also argued that jobs were destroyed when wages councils forced firms to pay more than they could afford. Downward pressure on wages was soon apparent in advertised job vacancies in former wages-council sectors. The average fall varied from 9 per cent in the clothing industry to as much as 22 per cent in hairdressing establishments.

Conclusion

The case for a national minimum wage in the UK remains controversial. It is clearly inconsistent with the Conservative government's belief in the efficacy of flexible labour markets. Nevertheless, advocates of a national minimum wage argue that there is a need to provide protection against low wages for employees who are in a weak bargaining position and who are, therefore, at the mercy of employers who take advantage of them. The potential costs of introducing a national minimum wage must be carefully weighed against the perceived benefits of protecting the weakest members of the labour market.

Chapter 7 discusses the European dimension to the issue.

KEY WORDS

Low pay	Trade boards
National minimum wage	Wages councils
Efficiency wage effect	Flexible pay determination
Shock effects	

Reading list

Gavin, M., and Swann, P., 'The minimum wage debate', *Economic Review*, February 1992.

Simpson, L., and Paterson, I., 'A national minimum wage for Britain?', *Economics*, spring 1992.

Wilkinson, M., Chapter 8 in *Equity and Efficiency*, Heinemann Educational, 1993.

Essay topics

1. (a) How can the differences between positive and normative economics be illustrated by reference to the proposal for a national minimum wage? [30 marks]
   (b) Examine the likely economic effects of the implementation of a national minimum wage. [70 marks]
   [University of London Examinations and Assessment Council 1993]
2. Why were minimum wages imposed in certain UK industries? What impact, if any, would you expect the abolition of wages councils to have on wages, employment and conditions in industries such as retailing or hairdressing? [20 marks]
   [Northern Examinations and Assessment Board, AS level, 1993]
3. (a) Explain the marginal revenue productivity theory of demand for labour in an industry. [10 marks]
   (b) Use this theory to discuss the possible effects on wages, and employment, of the introduction of a national minimum wage in the industry. [15 marks]
   [University of Cambridge Local Examinations Syndicate 1993]

Data Response Question 4

The hotel and catering industry

This task is based on a question set by the Associated Examining Board in 1993. Read extract A below which is adapted from an article by D. Kingman published in the *Wiltshire Times* on 29 November 1991. Extract B is based on a letter received by the newspaper in response to the article. Study both pieces and answer the questions.

Extract A – *Catering suffers from indigestion*

What a dismal tale is told of the local hotel and catering industry in November's Wiltshire Employment Update.

Pay for jobs offered is low – 35 per cent below national average earnings. And it is increasing at one per cent a year below the rise in the economy as a whole.

Jobs involve shift work, split shifts, weekend and evening work.
These unsocial hours are said to be a major cause of staff recruitment problems.

Less than 20 per cent of jobs offer flexible working hours and only 43 per cent offer a pension scheme.

Not surprisingly some 49 per cent of companies surveyed said they had recruiting difficulties particularly for trained chefs and waiters, followed by cleaners and receptionists.

One of the most frequent reasons given for these problems was the low status of catering in this country compared with the rest of Europe.

This is clearly an industry with its head buried deep in the sand. It could be that because it lacks competition it appears so complacent. It may be in for a jolt.

Competition for staff could be on its way. The go-ahead has already been given for a huge holiday village in the Cotswold Water Park on the county's northern boundary. Soon a decision will be taken on the similar Center Parcs project at Longleat. If approved, this will contain 600 villas and offer up to 750 jobs, similar to the Cotswold figure.

There could be 1500 jobs available, most of them in the hotel and catering market.

The only way to get them filled will be to pay over the odds, and Center Parcs will offer round-the-year employment as opposed to seasonal work.

Extract B – *Center Parcs jobs 'will not boost wage rates'*

Mr Kingman suggested that any increase in the number of jobs brought about by the development would lead to an improvement of wages and working conditions in the hotel and catering industry in Wiltshire. To recruit and retain workers things would have to improve. On balance he is probably wrong.

Firstly, Center Parcs, if it goes ahead, will need to remain competitive with other similar establishments in the UK.

If it decided that in order to attract enough local workers, wages would need to be raised by £1 an hour, then at least £1 million a year would be added to its wage bill. Couldn't this also lead to some of our existing hotels closing down?

Raising wages in a labour intensive industry is not consistent with remaining competitive.

Secondly, post 1992 a vast reservoir of unskilled labour, anxious to learn English and work here, will be available in Southern Europe. For a company with Center Parcs' pan European experience recruiting cheap labour from abroad will be no problem.

When I asked Center Parcs' managing director, how much he would be paying workers at the Longleat development he replied: "The going rate" which I took to mean £2.75 an hour which is what cleaners and cooks are paid in the local area.

South-West Wiltshire will have a declining number of young people in the 1990s. Perhaps Center Parcs may be relying on further changes to the Social Security system which could force more people who are at present able to claim benefits into taking very low wage jobs or face losing benefits.

1. Using the data, show how the demand for labour in the hotel and catering industry is a derived demand.   [4 marks]
2. Describe the factors that could affect the supply of labour to the hotel and catering industry.   [6 marks]
3. (a) Explain briefly how raising wage rates by £1 an hour could add at least £1 million a year to the wages bill of Center Parcs.   [2 marks]
   (b) Examine the possible effects on the local economy of this increase in wages.   [5 marks]
4. Using the data and economic theory, discuss how futur e wage levels in the hotel and catering industry in Wiltshire are likely to change. [8 marks]

Chapter Five
The aggregate labour market

*'Unemployment is a waste of our national resources, and this waste
can never be recovered. Unemployment is thus inefficient'.*
Andrew Clark and Richard Layard

The performance of an economy depends crucially on the *quality* of its
labour force and the level of employment. It is not suprising, therefore,
that industrialized countries are becoming increasingly concerned
about the continuing upward trend in the level of unemployment. As
Clark and Layard remind us, the UK is no exception. While the average rate of unemployment in the UK over the period 1942–66 was 1.1
per cent, this rose to 6.2 per cent over the period 1966–90.

Competitive model of the aggregate labour market
In this chapter we will be extending the competitive model introduced
in Chapter 2 to examine the factors influencing labour market equilibrium for the economy as a whole. We start by aggregating the quantity
of labour demanded and supplied by individual labour markets. The
fact that there will be significant differences between, for example, the
skills, location and mobility of different workers is for the moment
ignored.

The real wage rate
In the analysis of individual labour markets it was reasonable to
assume that all other prices and wages were fixed so that any change in
the money wage rate in the labour market under consideration implied
a change in the real wage rate. *Such an assumption is inappropriate
when examining the labour market for the economy as a whole.* An
increase in the money wage rate for the economy as a whole would,
given the productivity of labour, *cause the average price level to rise.*
In this case real wages might rise, fall, or stay the same, depending on
the relative changes in the money wage rate and the average price level.
The problem is resolved by making the quantity of labour demanded
and supplied a function of the **real wage rate** (the money wage rate
divided by the average price level).

Aggregate labour demand

In Figure 15 it is assumed that each worker in employment will work the same number of hours. This has the advantage of allowing us to define the quantity of labour in terms of the total number of workers employed. The aggregate labour demand curve (ALD) shows the total demand for labour at each real wage rate. *Profits will be maximized at the level of employment where the real wage rate is equal to the marginal physical product of labour.*

ALD slopes downward from left to right, indicating that the quantity of labour demanded is higher the lower the real wage rate. There are two reasons for this:

- First, as the real wage rate falls there will be a *substitution effect* in favour of employing more labour and against employing other resources because labour has become relatively cheaper.
- Secondly, as the real wage rate falls labour costs will fall relative to the price of the goods produced, thereby compensating for the fact that as more labour is employed the *marginal physical product* of labour falls, as predicted by the law of diminishing marginal returns.

Aggregate labour supply

The aggregate labour supply curve (ALS) shows the supply of labour *immediately* available for work at each real wage rate. The curve slopes upward from left to right, indicating that the number of workers willing and able to accept job offers increases the higher the real wage rate. This can be explained in terms of the increasing opportunity cost of remaining out of work as the real wage rate rises. *Empirical studies suggest that ALS is relatively inelastic with respect to the real wage rate.*

Aggregate labour force

The size of the labour force at each real wage rate is indicated by the aggregate labour force curve (ALF). It shows that more people of working age will be persuaded to join the labour force as the real wage rate rises. As discussed in Chapter 1, the decision of an individual whether to join the labour force or to opt for other non-market uses of time is influenced by a number of factors. These will include changes in the real value of market earnings.

The difference between ALS and ALF at each real wage rate consists of those members of the labour force who are unemployed for frictional or structural reasons and who are not, therefore, *immediately*

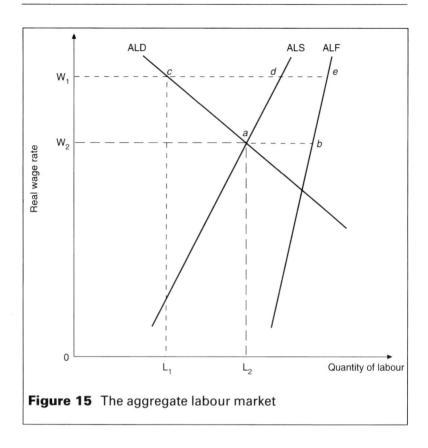

Figure 15 The aggregate labour market

available for work. When the real wage rate rises the gap between ALS and ALF will narrow. This can be explained by a fall in the **replacement ratio**. The replacement ratio is the ratio of real diposable income out of work to real disposable income in work. Thus when real wages increase relative to unemployment and other benefits, this causes the replacement ratio to fall so that there is a greater incentive for members of the labour force to make themselves *immediately* available for work.

Equilibrium level of employment

In a competitive market where money wages and prices are flexible, real wages must also be flexible. Basic supply and demand theory tells us that market forces will ensure an equilibrium real wage rate at W_2 and an equilibrium level of employment at L_2. When the aggregate labour market is in equilibrium the aggregate demand and supply of labour are equal, and all workers willing and able to work at the prevailing real wage rate can find employment. To economists this means that there is **full employment**. Some members of the aggregate labour force will remain unemployed (*b* minus *a*) for frictional or structural reasons.

FRICTIONAL AND STRUCTURAL UNEMPLOYMENT

Not all persons unemployed and seeking employment are available for work at any given moment. In the absence of perfect information regarding the availability of employment opportunities, some may prefer not to accept the first job that becomes available, but to remain unemployed and continue searching in the hope of finding a better one, perhaps offering a higher wage, pleasanter conditions or work more in keeping with their skills. In any dynamic economy some industries will be expanding whilst others are contracting and consequently there will always be individuals moving from one job to another. This kind of unemployment is called **frictional unemployment**. If individuals always moved from one job to another instantaneously frictional unemployment would be eliminated. In some cases individuals who find themselves unemployed as a result of industrial decline in one sector of the economy may lack the skills necessary to obtain employment in an expanding sector. For example, vacancies may be available for housebuilders while car assembly plant workers are unemployed. Alternatively there may be job vacancies in one region of the economy which is expanding and unemployment in a different region which is contracting. This kind of unemployment is called **structural unemployment**. It can cause serious problems when individuals are unable or unwilling to learn new skills or move to areas where job vacancies exist. Long-term unemployment may result.

The New Classical argument

The New Classical theory of the aggregate labour market adopts the view that, in the absence of *institutional constraints* such as trade union power or minimum-wages legislation, the real wage rate will always adjust to give equilibrium between aggregate labour supply and demand. However, where there are *institutional constraints* which fix money wages so that the real wage rate is above the equilibrium level, the level of employment will be reduced. If, for example, the real wage rate in Figure 15 was fixed at W_1 (a real wage floor), this would reduce the level of full employment to L_1 and the aggregate supply of labour would exceed the aggregate labour demand by $(d - c)$. This is called **classical unemployment**. Note that when the real wage rate is increased to W_1 the level of frictional and structural unemployment falls to $(e - d)$, giving total unemployment of $(e - c)$. According to the New Classical argument the economy is always at full employment and unemployment is always voluntary.

The natural rate of unemployment

Classical plus frictional and structural unemployment as a percentage of the aggregate labour force is called the **natural rate of unemployment**, otherwise known as the **non-accelerating inflation rate of unemployment – NAIRU**.

With this view of the labour market, increasing the level of employment is accomplished by using **supply-side policies** to reduce the natural rate of unemployment. *New Classical economists emphasize the efficiency of freely operating markets and advocate policies which remove, or at least reduce, the effects of market imperfections.* The most obvious target for attack is classical unemployment where the theory quite clearly indicates that the removal of the *institutional constraints* would allow market forces to secure an equilibrium real wage rate at W_2 in Figure 15 and an equilibrium level of employment at L_2. Unemployment would fall from $(e - c)$ to $(b - a)$, reducing the natural rate of unemployment to its frictional and structural components.

Supply-side policies

Any supply-side policy which increases the demand for labour (i.e. shifts ALD to the right) or increases the supply of labour (i.e. shifts ALS to the right) will further reduce the natural rate of unemployment and increase the level of full employment by curtailing the remaining frictional and structural unemployment.

The *aggregate demand* for labour would respond to policies designed to:

- increase the productivity of workers by investment in new capital, the development of new technology and investment in training and education
- encourage employers to offer more jobs to the long-term unemployed by introducing work trial schemes and employment grants, and by reducing national insurance payments.

The *aggregate supply* of labour would respond to policies designed to:

- remove disincentives to work such as high marginal rates of personal taxation, and unemployment and supplementary benefits which are high relative to the equilibrium real wage rate
- reduce the mismatch between unemployed workers and available jobs by increasing geographical and occupational flexibility
- reduce the costs of searching for employment by providing work experience and help in looking for work.

There is an important difference to be noted between the outcome of supply-side policies designed to increase ALD and those designed to increase ALS.

As Figure 16 illustrates, an increase in ALD to ALD_1, *ceteris paribus*, results in the equilibrium level of full employment rising to L_3 and an

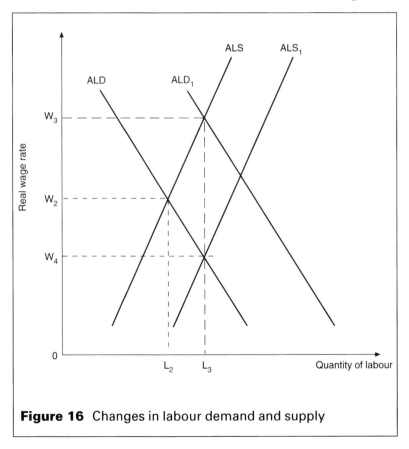

Figure 16 Changes in labour demand and supply

The theory is right, but will jobs package work?

DOUGLAS McWILLIAMS AND
MARK PRAGNELL

With a week proving to be a long time in politics, it is becoming difficult to remember that the centrepiece of the 1994 Budget was a package of 12 separate measures to reduce unemployment.

Normally when a series of measures are packaged together like this it reflects either an attempt in Whitehall to give measures of individual unimportance sufficient scale to merit a headline or an inability to decide between completing claims for funding ending in a messy compromise to share the money out.

But this package is different. In the past ten years, research into the causes of persistently high unemployment in the UK and elsewhere in Europe has come up with useful information about the causes. What is impressive about the Budget package is how closely it reflects the results of this research.

The expansion of the Work Trial scheme, which allows employers to take on at no cost those unemployed for more than six months for a three-week trial period, is an attempt to bring the outsiders in by bridging the information gap. It gives employers the chance to find out how good potential recruits are before they have to pay for them.

The Budget also included measures that recognise the problems faced by employers when hiring the long-term unemployed. The 0.6 per cent cut in employers' National Insurance contributions for all employees earning less than £205 a week and the one-year NI holiday for firms employing those jobless for more than two years both reduce the hiring costs that make firms reluctant to employ new workers. The pilot Workstart Schemes, which will benefit about 5,000 people at a cost to the Treasury of £8 million, will compensate employers for their hiring costs by providing grants for those who take on the long-term unemployed.

The new arrangements for payment of NI and PAYE quarterly rather than monthly will also reduce the administrative burden of job creation for small firms.

The Budget increased funding for programmes to alleviate the costs of searching for employment. Community Action attempts to reduce the search costs of 4,000 long-term unemployed by providing work experience and help in looking for work. The Jobseekers Allowance will provide direct compensation for search costs faced by the unemployed and will penalise those who do not actively hunt for work. The national extension of 1-2-1 interviews and Workwise courses target the particular problems that face jobseekers aged between 18 and 24.

The measures to ease the transition into work are clear attempts to reduce the job acceptance costs faced by the long-term unemployed. The decision to exempt the Back-to-Work Bonus from tax means the long-term unemployed will receive greater compensation for the costs they face. The Jobfinder's Grant, an average payment of £200 to those unemployed for more than two years who find work, tries "to cover start-up costs". Improvements in the payment of family credit and the four-week honeymoon for rent and council tax support help to mitigate a major job acceptance cost: the cost of losing social security benefits.

It may appear that even if these measures work, they will only recycle the unemployed, with long-term unemployed taking jobs that might otherwise be taken by those who had been unemployed for shorter periods. But the insider–outsider analysis suggests that, even if this is the initial effect, in the longer term the presence of more insiders in the labour market increases competition for jobs and improves the trade-off between inflation and unemployment. This in turn will result in the ability to run the economy at lower rates of unemployment without risks of inflation.

The Times, 29 December 1994

increase in the real wage rate to W_3. *This is the high-skill high-real-wage option which relies on an increase in worker productivity that comes from new capital investment, new technology and education and training programmes.*

An increase in ALS to ALS_1, *ceteris paribus*, also increases the equilibrium level of employment to L_3 by reducing frictional and structural unemployment. However, in this case there is a *reduction* in the real wage rate to W_4. *This is the low-skill low-wage option which relies on increasing flexibility in the labour market and incentives for unemployed members of the labour force to seek immediate employment.* Too much flexibility may be the cause of serious poverty problems (see the box, 'The trouble with success'). There is growing evidence that while government policy in the UK is concentrating on increasing labour market flexibility the market itself has not been very successful in increasing the long-run growth in labour productivity. Nigel Healey explores the growth of labour productivity and the UK performance in his book *Supply Side Economics* in the series.

The Keynesian argument

An alternative view of the aggregate labour market is provided by Keynesian economists who argue that, even in the absence of *institutional constraints* on the money wage rate, it may not be possible – at least not in the short run – for market forces to ensure equilibrium between aggregate labour supply and demand.

> ' There may exist no expedient by which labour as a whole can reduce its real wage to a given figure by making revised money bargains with the entrepreneurs.' John Maynard Keynes

This will be the case either where money wages are slow to respond to changes in the labour market – wages are said to be *sticky* in these circumstances – or where changes in money wage rates result in corresponding changes in the average price level. In either case the adjustment in real wages necessary to restore equilibrium will not occur and, in the absence of government intervention, disequilibrium will continue – giving **cyclical unemployment**.

Cyclical unemployment, otherwise known as demand-deficient or Keynesian unemployment, begins with a fall in the level of aggregate demand for goods and services – perhaps as a result of a downturn in business expectations, or perhaps as the result of a deliberate policy to reduce inflation. This in turn results in a fall in the average price level relative to the money wage rate. Consequently, real wages increase. Assuming that the aggregate labour market had previously been in

The trouble with success

Europe and America look admiringly at each other's labour markets. Europe's are better at avoiding poverty; America's create far more jobs. Yet both are grappling with a common problem: how to provide a decent standard of living for those who lack marketable skills

Many Europeans are bemused by the interest that the Clinton administration is showing in their policies on employment and unemployment. So intrigued by the European model are Bill Clinton and his labour secretary, Robert Reich, that America is hosting a "jobs summit" in Detroit on March 14th–15th – a rare opportunity for labour ministers to share ideas (and limelight). Europe's bemusement is easy to explain. For years America has been far better at creating new jobs and holding aggregate unemployment in check. Europe may have much to learn from America on this subject – but what, you could be forgiven for asking, can Europe teach America?

The charts opposite show two faces of America's labour market. Chart 1 tracks employment as a proportion of 15–64-year-olds in America and Europe. The proportion of people in employment is less susceptible to confusion and obfuscation than "unemployment". In 1973, as it happens, roughly 65% of the working-age populations in both Europe and America were in work. By the early 1990s the overall employment rate had increased substantially in America (to about 72%) and fallen somewhat in Europe (to 62%).

Moreover, America's smaller burden of aggregate unemployment is more spread around, so that spells of joblessness are shorter. Roughly half of America's unemployed find work within a month; only about 5% of Europe's unemployed do.

Chart 2 explains part of the reason why Americans are less impressed by this than Europeans. It shows the earnings of workers in the highest and lowest deciles of the income distibution as a proportion of median earnings. A European in the lowest decile earns 68% of median European pay. His American counterpart earns just 38% of median American pay. In terms of purchasing power, low-income Europeans earn 44% more per hour than low-income Americans; low-income Germans earn more than twice as much.

America's labour market delivers more employment and, therefore, more output and higher average living standards than Europe's; but the price is worse poverty in and out of work, and greater economic insecurity. This is not an accidental conjunction. America's harsh benefits system, which threatens the unemployed with poverty, and then delivers on the threat, is a crucial reason why America suffers less from unemployment in general, and from long-term unemployment in particular. In a labour market in which wages can fall to whatever level is needed to match supply and demand, an impressive rate of job creation is to be expected.

Source: *The Economist*, 12 March 1994

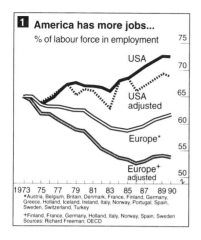

1 **America has more jobs...**

% of labour force in employment

USA

USA adjusted

Europe*

Europe+ adjusted

75
70
65
60
55
50

1973 75 77 79 81 83 85 87 89 90

*Austria, Belgium, Britain, Denmark, France, Finland, Germany, Greece, Holland, Iceland, Ireland, Italy, Norway, Portugal, Spain, Sweden, Switzerland, Turkey
+Finland, France, Germany, Holland, Italy, Norway, Spain, Sweden
Sources: Richard Freeman; OECD

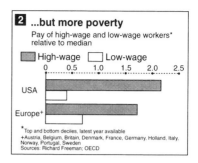

2 **...but more poverty**

Pay of high-wage and low-wage workers* relative to median

▨ High-wage ☐ Low-wage

0   0.5   1.0   1.5   2.0   2.5

USA

Europe+

*Top and bottom deciles, latest year available
+Austria, Belgium, Britain, Denmark, France, Germany, Holland, Italy, Norway, Portugal, Sweden
Sources: Richard Freeman; OECD

These charts refer to the *Economist* article opposite

equilibrium, the outcome of the fall in aggregate demand is a move to disequilibrium. With sticky wages, market forces will not be able to quickly restore equilibrium in the aggregate labour market. *The result is a level of employment which is below full employment and a rate of unemployment which is above the natural rate.* Again the argument can be illustrated with the aid of Figure 15. A fall in the level of aggregate demand results in an increase in the real wage rate from W_2 to W_1, giving cyclical unemployment of $(d - c)$. The level of employment falls to L_1.

While the effect may be similar to that resulting from *institutional constraints* which cause classical unemployment, which is described above, the cause and the policy implications of cyclical unemployment are quite different. Furthermore, it should be noted that while classical unemployment is *voluntary* and part of the natural rate of unemployment, cyclical unemployment is *involuntary* and is additional to the natural rate.

The failure of money wage rates to respond to a change in labour market conditions could be due to:

- wage contracts between employers and employees which cannot be changed in the short term
- insider/outsider situations where wage negotiations are undertaken by workers in employment who may not wish to accept lower money wages in order to increase employment opportunities for outsiders (and so self-interest rules).

We'll have to lay off some workers – supply has exceeded demand.

Macroeconomic policies

The Keynesian solution to unemployment problems which result from a fall in the aggregate demand for goods and services is to use macro-economic policy to boost the level of economic activity. By making use of expansionary fiscal and monetary policy, Keynesians argue that aggregate demand will be increased, which in turn will lead to an increase in the quantity of labour demanded.

One of the problems of this policy, and a reason why recent govern-ments in the UK have been reluctant to use it, is the risk of increasing the rate of inflation. Nevertheless, many economists have argued that the government is wrong to reject the use of demand management to deal with situations where the actual rate of unemployment has risen above the natural rate. The alternative of relying on market forces to resolve the problem is that cyclical unemployment may persist with all the social and economic costs that implies.

UK labour market policy

Aggregate labour market policy in the UK since 1979 has been very much along the lines proposed by the New Classical economists. The objective has been to strengthen market forces by increasing the incentives for workers to seek out productive activities and to remove market imperfections which constrain its operation. The policies have included:

- legislative changes, designed to remove the rigidities in the labour market imposed by the activities of trade unions (see Chapter 3) and wages councils (see Chapter 4)
- changes to the tax and social security system designed to increase incentives to work
- steps to improve the occupational and geographical mobility of labour in order to reduce the structural and frictional consequences of mismatch.

Since 1979 the marginal rate of income tax paid by top earners has been reduced from 83 per cent to 40 per cent, one of the lowest top rates in Europe. The basic rate has also been cut from 33 to 25 per cent. A new bottom rate of 20 per cent was introduced in 1989. Whether these changes will eventually lead to an increase in the aggregate supply of labour only time will tell. Research undertaken prior to 1979, and subsequent research undertaken following the changes in the 1980s, suggests that no significant effect can be expected. However, more recent research undertaken by Professors Layard, Nickell and Jackman, which is examined in more detail below, indicates that the natural rate of unemployment in the latter part of the 1980s would have been 0.3 per cent higher without the tax changes.

Unemployment trap

In the case of the **unemployment trap** individuals have a financial disincentive to seek work. The replacement ratio, which was defined earlier in this chapter, provides an indicator of the potential disincentive effect. As the replacement ratio approaches unity, so the disincentive to work becomes greater. In the case of the unemployment trap the replacement ratio is close to or exceeds unity, indicating that disposable income in work is only just above or even less than disposable income out of work. Economists such as Professor Minford have argued that even in less extreme cases, over-generous unemployment benefits lead to a lengthening of the period of job search and a reluctance to take on immediately available low-paid jobs by workers who are unemployed for frictional or structural reasons.

Changes in the social security system have given rise to a reduction in

---

WORKFARE

In the United States of America, reluctance on the part of some workers to take on available low-paid jobs has resulted in the enforcement of **workfare** programmes. Individuals in receipt of welfare benefits, who are identified as being able to work, are helped to find jobs and required to work as a condition of receiving government support. Some states have been operating workfare programmes since the 1960s. However, workfare has not been very successful, partly because social workers have sometimes been reluctant to force their clients to work, but also because of the problems and costs of finding jobs and monitoring performance.

---

the number of people in work with high replacement ratios over the past fifteen to twenty years. In particular the far-reaching reforms in the structure of social security benefits, which were introduced in April 1988, accentuated and continued the declining trend. However, the cyclical downturn in the economy in the early 1990s has resulted in a slight upturn. A major factor which helped to improve replacement ratios was the introduction in 1988 of Family Credit, designed to help the families of low-income, full-time workers.

A full discussion of the UK social security arrangements is provided by David Whynes in his book, *Welfare State Economics* in the series.

The **Restart Programme**, which was introduced in 1986, is also aimed at reducing the level of frictional and structural unemployment. This programme has three main components:

- to provide special guidance for the long-term unemployed
- to encourage the long-term unemployed to put more effort into job searching
- to persuade the long-term unemployed to accept job offers more readily.

The Restart Programme has been supplemented by subsequent changes which remove the right to unemployment benefit from any unemployed worker who refuses to accept a 'reasonable' job offer, even though the new job may be lower paid. More recently, the **Jobseekers Allowance** announced in the Autumn 1994 Budget will replace unemployment benefit, reducing the period of payments from twelve months to six, after which those still without work will become eligible for means-tested benefits.

The natural rate of unemployment

Research undertaken by Professors Layard, Nickell and Jackman and published in their book *Unemployment* (Oxford University Press, 1991), has shown that the natural rate of unemployment in the UK – or the equilibrium unemployment rate as they prefer to call it – has increased dramatically over the last 25 years. The details are given in Figure 17.

This indicates that the natural rate of unemployment was less than 3 per cent throughout the 1950s and 1960s, but rose above 7 per cent in the 1970s and 8 per cent in the 1980s. A peak was reached in 1984–86 at 9.9 per cent when the actual rate of unemployment was 11.3 per cent, before it fell back to 8.3 per cent in 1990 when the actual rate was 6.5 per cent. Their estimate for the long-run natural rate of unemployment, based on data available in 1990, was 8 per cent. Figure 17 shows that until 1973 the actual and natural rates of unemployment were closely related but have diverged in subsequent periods.

Layard, Nickell and Jackman' s investigation of the factors influencing the natural rate of unemployment confirm some of the arguments of the New Classical economists.

- Trade union power and the generosity of the social security system are cited as important factors pushing up the natural rate of unemployment over the early periods. The influence of trade union power reached a peak over the period from 1969–73 to 1974–80 but declined significantly after 1980.

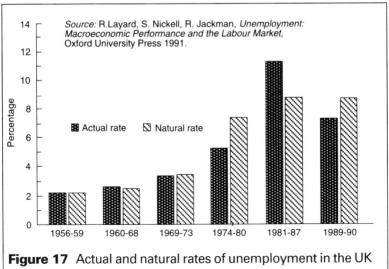

Figure 17 Actual and natural rates of unemployment in the UK

- Since 1986, changes in the social security system, particularly the Restart Programme under which conditions for receiving unemployment benefits were made more stringent, have resulted in a lower natural rate of unemployment than would otherwise have been the case.
- They also explain the impact that changes in the UK terms of trade have had on the natural rate of unemployment. In particular, in the 1970s and the 1980s the improvement in the terms of trade had a substantial adverse effect.
- In the period since 1980, North Sea oil has kept the natural rate of unemployment over 2.5 per cent lower than it would otherwise have been.

One factor which has had a continuing and increasing influence on the natural rate of unemployment has been the problem of *skills mismatch*. This has become an increasingly serious problem reflecting the high level of industrial restructuring since the early 1980s. This issue is taken up in the next chapter.

Conclusion

The actual rate of unemployment rose again after 1990, reaching a peak of 10.9 per cent in early 1993. Even though it has fallen more recently it remains a serious economic problem. Not only is unemployment a waste of resources, it is also a cause of great unhappiness and distress for the families of unemployed workers.

KEY WORDS

Real wage rate	Supply-side policies
Replacement ratio	Cyclical unemployment
Full employment	Unemployment trap
Frictional unemployment	Workfare
Structural unemployment	Restart Programme
Natural rate of unemployment	Jobseekers Allowance
Non-accelerating inflation rate of unemployment (NAIRU)	

Reading list

Bhattacharya, P., 'Unemployment' in Hare, P. and Simpson, L., *British Economic Policy*, Harvester Wheatsheaf, 1993.

Clark, A., and Layard, R., Chapter 2 in *UK Unemployment*, 2nd edn, Heinemann Educational, 1993.

Healey, N., Chapter 5 in *Supply Side Economics*, 3rd edn, Heinemann Educational, 1996.

Smith, D., Chapter 6 in *UK Current Economic Policy*, Heinemann Educational, 1994.

Whynes, D., *Welfare State Economics*, Heinemann Educational, 1992.

Essay topics

1. (a) Why is it difficult to agree what constitutes full employment? [10 marks]

   (b) Discuss the view that imperfections in the labour market are the main cause of unemployment in the United Kingdom. [15 marks]

   [Associated Examining Board 1993]

2. Compare Keynesian and supply-side policies for reducing unemployment. [25 marks]

   [Welsh Joint Education Committee 1993]

3. (a) What factors determine the level of aggregate supply in an economy? [40 marks]

   (b) To what extent may reductions in unemployment benefit and income tax rates affect the general level of unemployment? [60 marks]

   [University of London Examinations and Assessment Council 1993]

4. 'Wages are sticky downwards'. Assuming this to be true, how does the labour market adjust to changes in the demand for, and supply of, labour? [25 marks]

   [Oxford and Cambridge Schools Examination Board 1994]

5. (a) Explain what is meant by 'the natural rate of unemployment' (also known as NAIRU). [30 marks]

   (b) Evaluate the effects of demand-side and supply-side policies on the natural rate of unemployment. [70 marks]

   [University of London Examinations and Assessment Council 1995]

Data Response Question 5

'The dole'

This task is based on a question set by the University of London Examinations and Assessment Council in 1994. Read the following article which was published in the *Economist* on 28 September 1991 under the title 'The cursed dole', and then answer the questions.

Today's tolerance would have astonished people in the 1960s. This week a new book by three British economists considers what the profession has learnt about the subject over the past 20 years. *Unemployment: Macroeconomic Performance and Labour Market* convincingly refutes the idea that countries have no choice but to live with high unemployment.

The macroeconomics of unemployment looks discouraging. The evidence is clear that, for any economy, there is a rate of unemployment that is consistent in the long term with stable inflation. Economists call this the non-accelerating-inflation rate of unemployment, or NAIRU. "There is no long term trade-off between inflation and unemployment", a claim first made by Milton Friedman in the 1960s.

The trouble is that this stable inflation rate of unemployment may well be much too high; it need not correspond to "full employment". The challenge for governments, then, is to change the NAIRU. In the main, this is not a task for demand management, but for supply side policies.

The NAIRU, in effect, is the rate of unemployment that is just sufficient to control pressure for higher wages. It follows that, to lower the NAIRU, governments have to make unemployment more effective – so that a smaller amount of it will exert an equally powerful influence over wage setting. This can be done in several ways. They boil down to one broad idea: the unemployed must become stronger competitors in the labour market.

The new book says that "the unconditional payment of benefits for an indefinite period is clearly a major cause of high European unemployment". In Japan, unemployment benefits stop after six months. Benefits in most European countries are of virtually unlimited duration.

For years, Sweden's labour market policy has been the most successful in Europe. Benefits stop altogether after 14 months, but during that time the unemployed are helped to find work. The means include high quality training courses and recruitment subsidies (including a wage subsidy of up to 50% for those unemployed for more than six months). Sweden spends roughly seven times as much per unemployed worker on such measures as Britain – or roughly 1% of GDP. The net cost to taxpayers is small.

Policies that oblige and equip the unemployed to find jobs will work better if the labour market can be opened up to the new competition. That means scrapping all minimum wage laws. It also means curbing union power. Unemployment is lower if unions and employers co-ordinate their wage bargaining either across industries or nationally.

1. Examine and illustrate what is meant by the phrase 'There is no long term trade-off between inflation and unemployment'.
   [5 marks]
2. Explain what is meant when the author states that changing the non-accelerating inflation rate of unemployment 'is not a task for demand management, but for supply side policies'. [4 marks]
3. Using the passage, examine the statement 'the unconditional payment of benefits for an indefinite period is clearly a major cause of high European unemployment'. [4 marks]
4. How can Sweden spend heavily to help the unemployed but find there is only a small net cost to taxpayers? [2 marks]
5. What might be the economic effects of 'scrapping all minimum wage laws'. [5 marks]

Chapter Six
Labour mobility and training policies

'The critical skills gap facing employers in the 1990s is associated with the emergence of a new category of "knowledge worker" who will have higher level education and training qualifications; intellectual skills geared to problem solving and decision making; and the ability to shoulder various responsibilities in the workplace.'
Skills and Enterprise Network

As we saw in the previous chapter, structural unemployment occurs when there is a mismatch between the supply and demand for labour. We can identify two types of mismatch:

- **Geographical mismatch** arises when job vacancies occur in regions of the economy where new jobs are being created but the job seekers with appropriate skills and qualifications are located in other regions that are suffering relative decline.
- **Skills mismatch** arises when unemployment exists alongside job vacancies in the same area but where the job seekers lack the skills and training that the vacancies require.

Geographical mobility

Where geographical mismatch occurs there should be an incentive for members of the labour force to migrate from areas of relatively high unemployment to those regions of the economy where the rate of unemployment is lower and vacancies are more plentiful.

There should also be an incentive for firms experiencing difficulty recruiting employees to relocate in areas of relatively high unemployment where people with appropriate skills are available. When labour markets are flexible and wage rates adjust to reflect regional variations in the supply and demand for labour, the incentive for labour and firm mobility is strengthened. Labour will migrate to areas where wages are relatively high, whilst firms will seek out regions with lower wage rates.

In practice there are significant disincentives to the mobility of labour, not least the financial costs associated with moving and finding new accommodation and the intangible costs of leaving behind family and friends. In addition, wage rates do not quickly or fully respond to regional variations in unemployment rates. This can be partly explained by the fact that in some industries wages are still set nationally.

Nevertheless, research studies suggest that regional variations in vacancies and the overall rate of unemployment do influence the level and direction of internal migration.

MIGRATION FROM NORTH TO SOUTH

During the first half of the 1980s, the dramatic decline in the manufacturing sector throughout the UK was compensated for in part in the south of England by an expanding service sector (see *Deindustrialization* by Bazen and Thirlwall in this series). The result was an increasing gap between unemployment in the north and south. By 1984 unemployment in the south of England was 8.6 per cent and in the north 18.3 per cent. The regional unemployment differences over this period coincided with an increasing net internal migration into the south which peaked at over 69 000 in 1986. In the second half of the decade the decline in unemployment generally was associated with a fall in internal migration.

During the 1980s the government introduced a range of measures designed to encourage the mobility of labour, including changes in housing and pension arrangements. It was claimed that people who own their own homes would find it easier to move to a new job compared with households tied to subsidized rented accommodation. Similarly, it was claimed that occupational pension schemes made it difficult for individuals to change jobs without loss of pension rights.

- The 1980 Housing Act gave public sector tenants the right to buy their homes.
- From July 1987 employees acquired the right to join a personal pension scheme instead of staying in the full state scheme or the scheme operated by their employer.

Whilst the internal migration of labour might reduce the gap between the unemployment rates of prosperous and depressed regions, *the possibility also arises that it could make the situation worse.* This will be the case where the exodus consists of the more productive and better trained job seekers with new skills. In these circumstances, indigenous firms may be reluctant to expand – or even remain – in the high-unemployment areas, and new firms will be reluctant to move in, resulting in cumulative decline. Divergence rather than convergence would be the outcome of this scenario. Furthermore, for the areas of relative prosperity the inward migration of job seekers will place an increasing burden on their infrastructure.

The ways in which governments have attempted to deal with the problem of regional unemployment are discussed by David Smith in *UK Current Economic Policy* in this series.

Training

At the end of the previous chapter it was suggested that one factor that has had an increasing impact on the natural rate of unemployment in the UK is the problem of *skills mismatch*. Apart from the employment implications, skills deficiencies reduce a country's competitiveness and productive potential. The problems involved are discussed by Andrew Clark and Richard Layard in *UK Unemployment* in this series.

It is generally accepted that an important factor explaining the UK's relative economic decline has been the inadequacy of its vocational education and training provision, so that:

- some job seekers are unskilled – for example, unemployed school leavers may find themselves in this category – with basic weaknesses in literacy and numeracy
- some job seekers have the wrong skills as a result of changes in the structure of industry or because of technological advance.

The 1994 report of the Trade and Industry Committee, *Competitiveness of UK Manufacturing Industry,* argues that, with the development of new technology,

'*the jobs required to accommodate large numbers of unskilled workers are disappearing*'

'*employees will increasingly need new skills throughout their working lives*'.

However, the UK is not exceptional. There is evidence to show that during the 1980s all industrialized countries experienced a switch in labour demand away from unskilled towards more highly skilled jobs. *This has resulted in a rise in the unemployment rate of low-skilled relative to high-skilled workers.* Not only is the number of highly skilled jobs increasing at the expense of the number of low or unskilled jobs, but the skill requirements of a wide range of occupations is also changing.

'These newly redundant bank employees have got a lot to learn'

If the UK fails to address its increasing problem of skills mismatch, more skilled jobs will be lost to overseas competitors who put greater emphasis on vocational education and training. The UK will then be forced to rely on importing low-skill low-wage job opportunities to resolve its unemployment problem.

The percentage of the UK workforce with a university degree compares adequately with other European countries. Indeed, in recent years there has been a substantial increase in the number of students participating in higher education. However, there is a significant gap at the intermediate level. Whilst over 60 per cent of the German workforce had intermediate vocational qualifications at the end of the 1980s, the comparable figure for the UK was 25 per cent. Furthermore, it is often argued that the quality of vocational training has not been as high in the UK as it has been in other countries, notably Germany.

Clearly the increasing skill needs over the next decade constitute an important challenge to the providers of vocational education and training in the UK.

Current government policy is to leave training provision to market forces and the decisions of individuals and firms. However, there are a number of problems associated with this policy, including the way it should be financed and the related issue of the **free rider.**

These problems were previously experienced with the apprentice scheme operating in the 1950s and early 1960s. *Apprenticeship schemes were financed by individual companies which ran the risk of losing employees at the end of their apprenticeships to free riders – other firms that did not bear the training costs but were prepared to offer premium wages.*

Industry must invest in skill and technology says Portillo

British industry must invest in skill and technology if it is to compete successfully in expanding overseas markets, Michael Portillo, the Employment Secretary, said yesterday.

Mr Portillo was speaking to 2000 delegates at the annual conference of the Institute of Personnel and Development at Harrogate.

The Government aimed at creating an economy that could provide wages high enough to sustain a good standard of living, pay for public services, and raise the quality of life.

He said: "Low-wage economies present formidable competition but their wages are so much lower than ours, we cannot hope to compete by driving down our wage levels. We have to do something quite different, we have to climb the ladder of technology."

"That means enhancing Britain's competitive edge. We must create products which owe more to human knowledge than to human muscle ... our future lies in providing goods and services which have high added value because of their technology, design and innovation."

The Guardian, 27 October 1994.

A more planned approach was adopted following the 1964 Industrial Training Act under which an Industrial Training Board was established for each industrial sector. The boards were empowered to raise finance from firms within their industry to pay for training programmes – thus reducing the free rider problem. However, they were disbanded during the 1980s.

More recently the government has switched emphasis away from national and regional training needs to the needs of local labour markets. **Training and Enterprise Councils** (TECs) in England and Wales, and **Local Enterprise Councils** (LECs) in Scotland, are government funded voluntary organizations dominated by local employers. They are responsible for:

- ascertaining local skill needs
- encouraging local employers to train their employees
- implementing government training programmes for the unemployed.

A major criticism has been that much of the government funding is directed towards the needs of the unemployed and new entrants to the labour market. Insufficient provision is made from public funds to train the existing workforce.

In order to establish national standards for training qualifications the government established the **National Council for Vocational Qualifications** (NCVQ) in the late 1980s. The NCVQ is responsible for the accreditation of National Vocational Qualifications in England and Wales. In Scotland the **Scottish Vocational Education Council** has a similar responsibility for Scottish Vocational Qualifications. Since 1990, those employers who are deemed to be good trainers – committed to investing in the development of the skills of their employees – are eligible for the accolade **Investor in People**.

KEY WORDS

Geographical mismatch
Skills mismatch
Free rider
Training and Enterprise Councils
Local Enterprise Councils

National Council for Vocational
   Qualifications
Scottish Vocational Education
   Council
Investors in People

Reading list

Bazen, S., and Thirlwall, T., Chapter 5 in *Deindustrialization*, Heinemann, 1992.

Clark, A., and Layard, R., Chapter 1 in *UK Unemployment*, 2nd edn, Heinemann Educational Educational, 1993.

Healey, N., 'The north–south divide: has regional policy failed?', in Healey, N., (ed), *Britain's Economic Miracle*, Routledge, 1993.

Smith, D., Chapter 8 in *UK Current Economic Policy*, Heinemann Educational, 1994.

Essay topics

1. How does the analysis and classification of unemployment contribute to our understanding of how to deal with it? Compare government training schemes, increases in aggregate demand and cuts in real wages as ways of dealing with unemployment. [25 marks]
   [Northern Examinations and Assessment Board 1993]

2. Explain what is meant by the elasticity of supply of labour. What impact would you expect a successful programme of UK government-funded training schemes to have on labour supply and wages in the economy? [20 marks]
   [Northern Examinations and Assessment Board, AS level, 1993]

3. What factors contribute to the immobility of labour in the UK? How effective have government policies been since 1979 in improving the mobility of labour? [20 marks]
   [Joint Matriculation Board, AS Level, 1992].

4. 'Skilled workers always earn more than unskilled ones and there-fore they should finance their own training.' Evaluate the relative merits of the training of skilled workers being financed by firms, the government, or themselves. [25 marks]
[University of Oxford Delegacy of Local Examinations, new syl-labus specimen paper].

Data Response Question 6

Where are the new jobs?

This task is based on a question in a new–syllabus specimen paper from the University of Oxford Delegacy of Local Examinations. Study Table A which is taken from an article by P. Bassett entitled 'Studying recent form for the jobseekers handicap', published in the *Times* on 11 January 1994, and answer the questions that follow.

Table A Job changes, 1992–93

Occupation		Industry	
Top 10	(%)	*Top 10*	(%)
1. Travel attendants	+18	1. Domestic service	+12
2. Personal service workers	+17	2. Rubber and plastic processing	+10
3. Metal process workers	+13	3. Printing and publishing	+9
4. Textile operatives	+12	4. Insurance	+9
5. Childcarers	+12	5. Sea transport	+8
6. Transport managers	+10	6. Footware and clothing	+7
7. Routine process workers	+8	7. Water supply	+6
8. Specialist managers	+7	8. General public services	+6
9. Legal associates	+7	9. Railways	+6
10.Health workers	+6	10. Nuclear fuel production	+6
Bottom 10	(%)	*Bottom 10*	(%)
1. Metal making workers	-27	1. Man-made fibre-making	-100
2. Farm managers	-14	2. Coal mining	-38
3. Librarians	-12	3. Leather goods	-32
4. Construction workers	-11	4. Other mineral extraction	-23
5. Armed forces ranks	-11	5. Commissioning	-14
6. Buyers and brokers	-10	6. Fishing	-14
7. Printers	-10	7. Research and development	-11
8. Catering workers	-9	8. Electricity production/distribution	-11
9. Welders	-9	9. Forestry	-11
10. Associate professionals	-9	10. Diplomacy	-9

1. Explain why employment fell in any *one* of the industrial categories shown. [10 marks]
2. Explain why employment rose in any *one* of the occupational categories shown. [10 marks]

Chapter Seven

The European Union

'We have not successfully rolled back the frontiers of the state in Britain only to see them reimposed at a European level.'
Margaret Thatcher

The Social Charter

The **Single European Act** of 1986 committed the member states of the European Community to the introduction of a *single market* which would eliminate all internal barriers to the movement of goods, services, capital and labour between them.

In order to achieve this objective a system of majority voting was adopted, thereby removing the need for unanimity on a wide range of issues. Concern was expressed, however, that the increased competition which would result from the completion of the single market might have undesirable consequences for employees.

In particular, it was argued that the development of a single market might encourage **social dumping**. The problem of social dumping occurs when multinational companies locate in countries with low wages and weak employment protection legislation, and consequently exert downward pressure on labour standards in countries where wages are higher, social security provisions better and employment legislation stricter.

Furthermore, there was a desire to ensure fair treatment and reasonable protection for labour force participants throughout the countries of the European Community and thereby reduce their reluctance to accept structural and technological change. The impact of structural and technological change can be cushioned by appropriate social protection for displaced workers and the provision of adequate opportunities for retraining.

These concerns led to the appearance in 1989 of the European Commission's *Charter of Fundamental Social Rights*, which became known simply as the **Social Charter**. The Charter is not a legal document, but a declaration setting out what the Commission considered to be basic social and employment rights that it felt should be guaranteed across Europe.

**CHARTER OF FUNDAMENTAL SOCIAL RIGHTS
FOR WORKERS**

- Freedom of movement of workers, including the right to have access to jobs in other countries as a result of recognition of qualifications.
- Fair and equitable remuneration for all workers, enabling them to enjoy a decent standard of living.
- Improved living and working conditions, including a weekly rest period and annual paid leave.
- Adequate social protection and assistance for those losing their jobs or unable to work.
- Freedom to join, or not to join, professional associations or trade unions and the right to negotiate terms and conditions of employment through collective bargaining.
- Access to vocational training, if necessary throughout an individual's working life.
- Equal treatment for men and women, including access to jobs, training and career opportunities as well as pay.
- Rights relating to information, consultation and participation, particularly when organizational or technological change is under consideration.
- Adequate provisions for ensuring health and safety at work.
- Protection of children and adolescents, including a minimum working age, maximum working hours and entitlement to vocational training after leaving school.
- Retirement pensions that provide a decent standard of living for elderly persons.
- Provision to enable disabled people to be integrated into employment and society in general.

The UK government opposed the Social Charter. Its view was, and remains, that imposing legal obligations on employers to provide workers with certain standards and rights would reduce flexibility in the labour market. Labour costs would rise and firms would become less competitive internationally, leading to job losses. On the other hand, allowing market forces to operate as freely as possible, with only the minimum of government intervention, would improve competitiveness and encourage employment growth. It was this commitment to removing what were perceived to be hindrances to the free operation of markets that had been an important factor in the government's decision to restrict the powers of trade unions.

The Maastricht Treaty

In 1991, the heads of government of European Union countries reached agreement at Maastricht on a **Treaty on European Union**, but only after the exclusion of its **Social Chapter**. The Social Chapter extended majority voting on a wider range of employment-related matters than had been agreed in the Single European Act.

The UK government refused to sign the treaty unless the Social Chapter was dropped, arguing that majority voting on all employment issues would result in the imposition of regulations which Britain had previously opposed in the Social Charter.

The Social Chapter was removed from the treaty but a protocol was added to it stating that *all countries, other than Britain, wished to take action along the lines laid down in the Social Charter and had reached agreement to establish common social and employment legislation.* The Treaty on European Union came into force in November 1993.

However, the UK government's attempts to opt out of European-level regulation of labour market matters may turn out to be of little practical effect.

- Under the protocol procedure, a directive on European Works Councils was adopted in September 1994. The directive requires large enterprises operating in more than one member state of the European Union to keep their workforce informed regarding company activities and to consult them on issues affecting their employment. Although the UK is not covered by the directive, about a hundred British-owned multinationals are affected by it because of their operations elsewhere in Europe. One of them, United Biscuits, has already agreed to set up a works council for its entire European workforce, including those in Britain, and a number of others are in the process of doing the same.
- The UK government has, reluctantly had to accept a ruling by the House of Lords (1994) that part-time workers in the UK should have the same dismissal and redundancy rights as full-time employees. As the majority of part-time workers are women, to deny them the same privileges as full-time employees would, according to the Law Lords, contravene the European Union directives on equal treatment and equal pay which Britain accepted in the 1970s.
- In 1993 a Working Time Directive was adopted by majority vote as part of the European Union health and safety regulations. It limits the length of the working week for employees (including overtime) to a maximum of 48 hours and also stipulates a minimum of four weeks' paid annual leave. The UK government, however, is challenging its validity as a measure relating to health and safety, and is refusing to implement any part of the directive until the European Court of Justice gives a ruling.

Conclusion

The UK government's policy is one of trying to ensure the freest possible operation of the labour market. It is continuing to do all it can to try to prevent regulations it considers would have harmful effects on the economy being imposed by the European Union.

KEY WORDS

Single European Act Treaty on European Union
Social dumping Social Chapter
Social Charter

Reading list

Hill, B., Chapter 3 in *The European Union*, Heinemann Educational, 1994.

Thomas, D., 'The labour market and European social measures', in Atkinson, G.B.J. (ed), *Developments in Economics: An Annual Review*, Vol. 10, Causeway Press, 1994.

Essay topics

1. Will the creation of a single European market in 1992 lead to fundamental changes in Britain's economic relationship with the European Community? [25 marks]
   [Oxford & Cambridge Schools Examination Board 1990]
2. Define a market and explain why markets can improve economic welfare. Discuss how the Single European Market is intended to increase the economic welfare of member states. [25 marks]
   [Northern Examinations and Assessment Board 1992].
3. What are the implications for the British economy of the completion of the Single European Market? [25 marks]
   [Oxford & Cambridge Schools Examination Board 1992].

Data Response Question 7

Living standards in the EU
This task is based on a question set by the University of Cambridge Local Examinations Syndicate (at AS level) in 1993. Study Table A which is taken from a World Bank Development Report in 1991, and answer the questions that follow.

Table A GNP per head in the
European Community, 1989 ($US)

Belgium	16 220
Denmark	20 450
France	17 820
Germany (West)	20 440
Greece	5 350
Ireland	8 710
Italy	15 120
Luxembourg	18 500
Netherlands	15 920
Portugal	4 250
Spain	9 330
United Kingdom	14 610

1. With the aid of the data in Table A, examine the differences in living standards between the member states of the European Community. [8 marks]
2. Discuss the ways in which the European Community policies seek to reduce these differences. [12 marks]

Chapter Eight

Developments in the UK labour market

'The labour market is much more diverse than it used to be'
Robert Taylor

In this chapter we examine some of the trends in the UK labour market that have emerged during the last fifteen to twenty years and which are likely to continue during the rest of the 1990s.

Pay determination

There have been significant moves towards localizing and individualizing pay settlements, while collective pay bargaining has been in decline and limits on pay increases operate in the public sector.

The government has encouraged a move away from pay settlements at the national level towards more **local pay determination**. *Fixing pay at national level does not take account of the different circumstances of individual enterprises or of variations in the demand for labour and the cost of living in different parts of the country.* Consequently jobs are lost in high-unemployment regions when nationally agreed wage rates more closely reflect the influence of labour shortages in low-unemployment regions.

During the 1980s, employers began to make increasing use of **performance-related pay** schemes. Relating pay to individual merit is not a new idea. However, traditional schemes concentrated on an individual's personal qualities, whereas performance assessment places much greater emphasis on setting individual working objectives within the context of company goals. Unlike conventional incentive pay schemes, performance-related pay uses qualitative as well as quantitative assessments of the achievement of targets.

The pay of fewer people is now determined by collective bargaining. Approximately 72 per cent of all employees were covered by collective agreements in 1973. By 1984 this had fallen to 64 per cent and by 1990 to 47 per cent.

At the time of writing, an **incomes policy** is being operated in the public sector as a means of controlling wage increases and the rate of inflation. During 1993 a ceiling on public-sector annual pay increases of 1.5 per cent operated when private sector pay was rising by 4 per cent. In September 1993, the Chancellor of the Exchequer announced that the government's wages bill for the subsequent year would be frozen at the existing level. However, rather than directly restricting pay rises, the government has used cash limits – the imposition of firm ceilings on public expenditure – to control pay increases. The government has announced its intention to continue this policy for the time being. Some public sector employees have their wages determined by Pay Review Bodies – for example, nurses, doctors, and schoolteachers in England and Wales. However, these decisions are also subject to cash limits.

INCOMES POLICIES

An incomes policy, sometimes associated with price controls **(prices and incomes policy)**, provides a mechanism by which a government can attempt to control increases in wages and inflation in a market economy. There are many variations, voluntary or statutory, comprehensive or partial, fixed or flexible, and most combinations have been used with varying degrees of success in the UK. The general conclusion of researchers who have attempted to quantify the effects of incomes policies has been that, although some degree of success in restraining wages might be achieved while the policy is in operation – particularly a pay freeze – once the policy has ended wages rise rapidly to compensate for the period of restraint.

There are a number of problems associated with incomes policies. Two criticisms are particularly common:

- Incomes policies are inevitably doomed to failure because they attempt to defy the laws of supply and demand. The policies are more likely to be successful, and for a longer period of time, if employers and employees can be persuaded that it is in the interests of their future prosperity and the cooperation of trade unions can be obtained.
- Incomes policies create rigidities and distortions in the labour market, affecting the way in which labour is allocated between expanding and contracting industries.

The growing importance of local pay determination and the decline in national agreements will make it increasingly difficult for future governments to use incomes policies, especially in the private sector.

Labour flexibility

The use and deployment of labour by firms has become increasingly more flexible. This has affected not only the range of tasks that individual workers may be required to undertake, but also the working-time and contractual arrangements they may have with their employers.

- The need for greater cost-effectiveness in an increasingly competitive world led many employers during the 1980s to expect their employees to perform any tasks within their capabilities when instructed to do so. Traditional demarcation lines were dropped as a result of work being reorganized, with trade unions in most cases accepting the need for increased **task flexibility**.

- Companies are increasingly devising working-time arrangements to suit their business needs. As a result, **shiftwork** is on the increase and so is the variety of shift patterns. **Part-time work** has also increased. The use of part-time workers reduces labour costs as workers are only employed when they are needed, often at lower wage rates than full-time employees. **Flexitime** arrangements allow employees to vary their daily hours of work as long as the agreed weekly or monthly total is achieved; and **annual hours arrangements** – which allow the employer to vary the number of hours worked by employees in the short term, subject to an agreed yearly total – are becoming more common.

- Many companies have been moving away from the idea that all work will be carried out by permanent employees. Economists now distinguish between **peripheral and core employees**. *Core employees* are permanent and generally full-time, undertake essential and regular work, and are needed to provide the organization with continuity. *Peripheral employees* are those hired to perform specific tasks for a particular time period. They enable firms to have a numerically flexible labour force that is responsive to short-term fluctuations in economic and other circumstances.

Employment in manufacturing and services

For over thirty years the UK, like most other developed countries, has experienced a period of **deindustrialization**. The definition, causes and consequences of deindustrialization are described by Stephen Bazen and Tony Thirlwall in a book in this series. They cite as the 'two best definitions of deindustrialization':

- a declining *share* of manufacturing in total employment, and
- an *absolute* decline in employment in manufacturing.

Employment in manufacturing as a share of total British employment fell from 36 per cent in 1960 to 20 per cent in 1993. The number of persons employed in the manufacturing sector fell from its peak of 9.5 million in the early 1960s to 4.25 million in 1993. The most rapid period of decline was between 1979 and 1982 when some 1.3 million manufacturing jobs were lost. Traditional manufacturing industries, such as motor vehicles and parts, metal manufacturing, textiles, leather, footwear and clothing all experienced reductions in employment of over 50 per cent during the period 1972–90 (Bazen and Thirlwall, Chapter 2).

While the manufacturing sector has witnessed a continuing decline in employment opportunities, employment in the service sector has grown in both absolute and relative terms. From less than 9.5 million employees in the early 1960s, service sector employment grew to 15.5 million in 1993 – 73 per cent of total employment in Britain. Since 1982, transport and communication employment has declined, but all other service sector industries have expanded, most notably banking and insurance, business services, and welfare and community services.

Women in employment

The number of women in employment increased from 9.1 million in 1975 to 10.6 million in 1994 (see Figure 18). This compares with a decline in the number of men in employment from 13.5 million to 10.8 million over the same period.

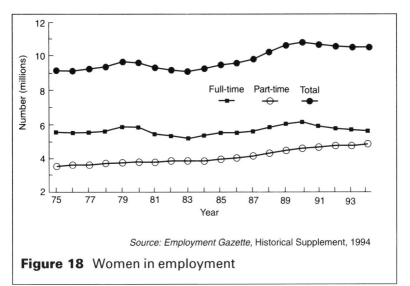

Source: *Employment Gazette,* Historical Supplement, 1994

Figure 18 Women in employment

There are a number of explanations for this increase. First, in addition to the prospect of increasing family income and the increasing percentage of single, separated and divorced women, changing attitudes of women and employers are important factors. The percentage of women prepared to forgo their careers while their children are young, and the level of discrimination by employers against women, are both in decline.

Secondly, women are economically active in most occupations. Nevertheless, gender-based job segregation continues to dominate the labour market, with women working predominantly in the service sector.

Thirdly, to a large extent the increase in female employment has been in part-time jobs. While 39 per cent of women in employment were in part-time jobs in 1975, this increased to 46 per cent by 1994. In certain occupations – for example, retailing, catering, the hotel industry and in some social and personal services – part-time work has become the norm.

Trade union mergers
The substantial fall in union membership since 1979 has caused significant financial problems for many unions. One of the results of this has been an increasing number of trade union mergers.

Between 1988 and 1993, fifty small unions simply transferred their members to much bigger unions and ceased to exist. Such mergers enabled small unions to escape from a vicious circle of falling membership and declining income.

Several amalgamations of large unions have taken place in recent years with the objective of achieving economies of scale and establishing a sound basis for further growth and development (see the boxed item).

TRADE UNION AMALGAMATIONS

Five trade unions with more than 250 000 members have been formed as a result of amalgamations since 1987. Their names and present sizes are:

Manufacturing, Science and Finance (MSF) – 552 000
Graphical, Paper and Media Union (GPMU) – 275 000
Amalgamated Engineering and Electrical Union (AEEU) – 835 000
Unison –1 400 000
Communication Workers Union (CWU) – 289 000

If present trends continue, by the end of the century the trade union movement in the UK could be dominated by three or four **superunions**, each with more than a million members. One such superunion is Unison, formed in 1993 as a result of a merger of three other unions (Nalgo, Nupe and Cohse). Its members are employed mainly in local government, the health service, the gas, electricity and water industries, transport and higher education.

Conclusion

Diversity seems to be the keynote of the labour market of the 1990s. There is much greater variety than there was a generation ago in the basis on which employees are hired, expected to work and rewarded. Gone are the days when nearly all work was done by full-time employees working a standard week with fixed starting and stopping times. Standard rates of pay throughout whole industries are becoming the exception rather than the rule and relating pay to individual achievement is commonplace. Many women are doing jobs which at one time were effectively closed to them. Trade union mergers are resulting in some large unions with diverse memberships. Britain is experiencing profound changes in the world of work.

KEY WORDS

Local pay determination	Part-time work
Performance-related pay	Flexitime
Incomes policy	Annual hours arrangements
Prices and incomes policy	Peripheral and core employees
Task flexibility	Deindustrialization
Shiftwork	Superunions

Reading list

Bazen, S., and Thirlwall, T., *Deindustrialization*, 2nd edn, Heinemann Educational, 1992.

National Institute of Economic and Social Research, Chapter 2 in *The UK Economy*, 3rd edn, Heinemann Educational, 1995.

Essay topics

1. Assess the case for and against replacing national collective bargaining with an alternative system such as regional bargaining or profit-related pay as a method of determining wages. [25 marks] [Associated Examining Board 1992]
2. What is the purpose of an incomes policy? For what reasons might a UK government be reluctant to use such a policy? [20 marks] [Joint Matriculation Board, AS level, 1992]
3. (a) Examine the arguments for and against a pay freeze in the public sector when an economy is suffering from inflationary pressure. [70 marks]
(b) Why would a pay freeze in the private sector be difficult to implement? [30 marks]
[University of London Examinations and Assessment Council 1995]

Data Response Question 8

Changing labour market conditions
This task is based on a new-syllabus specimen paper from the Associated Examining Board. Study all the data and then answer the questions.

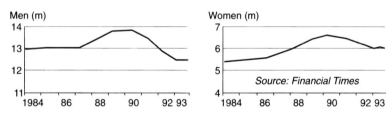

Figure A Full-time employment in the UK (seasonally adjusted)

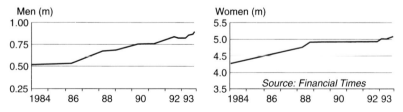

Figure B Part-time employment in the UK (seasonally adjusted)

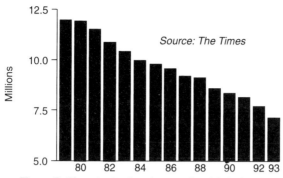

Figure C Changing trade union membership in the UK

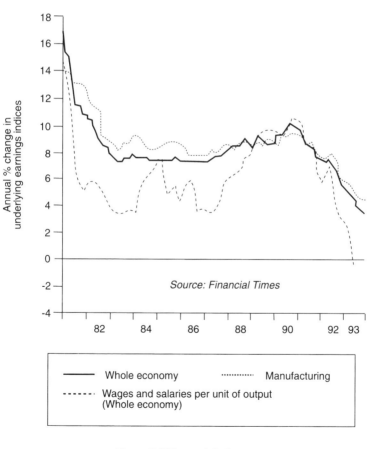

Figure D UK wage inflation

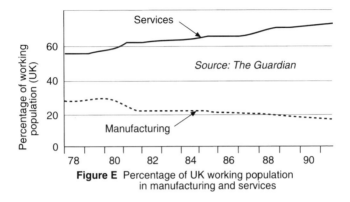

Figure E Percentage of UK working population in manufacturing and services

Table A Job changes in industry, 1992–93

Top 10	(%)
1. Domestic service	+12
2. Rubber and plastic processing	+10
3. Printing and publishing	+9
4. Insurance	+9
5. Sea transport	+8
6. Footware and clothing	+7
7. Water supply	+6
8. General public services	+6
9. Railways	+6
10. Nuclear fuel production	+6
Bottom 10	(%)
1. Man-made fibre-making	-100
2. Coal mining	-38
3. Leather goods	-32
4. Other mineral extraction	-23
5. Commissioning	-14
6. Fishing	-14
7. Research and development	-11
8. Electricity production/distribution	-11
9. Forestry	-11
10. Diplomacy	-9

Source: *The Times*, 11 January 1994

1. Describe the main changes in the pattern of male and female employment in the UK over the period shown by the data in Figures A and B. [3 marks]
2. Account for the decline in trade union membership in the UK shown in Figure C. [6 marks]
3. Discuss how changing labour market conditions may explain the changes in the rate of wage inflation in the UK shown in Figure D. [13 marks]
4. Explain the changes in the distribution of employment between manufacturing and service industries shown in Figure E and Table A. [13 marks]

Conclusion

In writing this short book on the UK labour market we set ourselves three main objectives.

- The first was to provide an introduction to the economic principles of supply and demand in the labour market.
- The second was to show how these principles can be used to analyse the impact of labour market policy.
- The third was to examine some of the many labour market developments that have taken place in recent years.

Since 1979, government policy has been to make the labour market more flexible, and hence more responsive to changes in labour supply and demand.

- The reduction of the power of trade unions, the abolition of wages councils and the move from national to local bargaining has resulted in greater wage flexibility.
- Deregulation of the labour market has resulted in the introduction of more flexible working conditions and hours and in particular a rapid expansion of part-time employment.
- Improved information systems have reduced the period of job search, and through training and education it is possible to acquire new skills on a continuing basis. Such measures are aimed at reducing frictional and structural unemployment by making more unemployed workers available for work as quickly as possible.
- Changes in the tax and benefit system have been directed towards increasing incentives to work by ensuring that workers are better off in work then they would be out of work.

The success of this policy will ultimately be measured not only in terms of the increased employment opportunities that are created, but also in terms of its impact on the quality of working life.

Index